# THE BOOK IN

# GERMANY

Other relevant Merchiston Publishing titles:

edited Alistair McCleery, *Images and Advertising*

edited Alistair McCleery and Benjamin A. Brabon, *The Influence of Benedict Anderson*

edited Alistair McCleery and Benjamin A. Brabon, *Scottish Comics* (2010)

edited Alistair McCleery and Benjamin A. Brabon, *The Influence of Don MacKenzie* (2010 forthcoming)

# THE BOOK IN GERMANY

edited by M.C. Fischer and W.A. Kelly

MERCHISTON PUBLISHING 2010

MERCHISTON PUBLISHING
Scottish Centre for the Book,
Edinburgh Napier University,
Craighouse Campus,
Edinburgh EH10 5LG
Publication Manager: Padmini Ray Murray

First published 2010

ISBN: 978-0-9553561-6-2

Printed and bound in Great Britain by Scotprint, Edinburgh

# CONTENTS

# Preface

The Scottish Centre for the Book, which will celebrate its fifteenth anniversary in 2010, acts as a focus for research into and scholarship in print culture and the sociology of texts. It hosts seminars and conferences and issues publications relating to the past, present and future of the printed word, its creation, diffusion and reception. Within such a broad remit, the Centre has specialised in three major areas: contemporary publishing, readership and the book trade in Scotland; the general history of the book in Scotland; and, through the SAPPHIRE initiative, the oral testimonies of those in Scotland who have worked in trades and professions linked to books during the course of the last century. We have also carried out a number of commissioned research projects related to the publishing industry, the creative industries in general, and the cultural heritage of Scotland.

The qualifying term 'Scottish' in our title, the Scottish Centre for the Book, however, while it rightly stresses that we have a particular concern for a distinctive Scottish tradition in writing, publishing and reading, does not imply an exclusivity of perspective or of interest. Current members of the Centre themselves originate from China, Germany, India, Italy, Poland, Spain (Catalonia) and the USA in addition to those from the constituent nations of the UK: England, Ireland, Scotland and Wales. As might be expected from such a heterogeneity, they research and publish on a wide range of topics drawn from an international palette.

One of these topics, identified primarily with the two editors of this volume, Mary Fischer and William Kelly, is the history of the book in Germany, from the manuscript period to the present. Thanks to their initiative, a very successful seminar on that topic was held at the National Library of Scotland in May 2008, supported by the Consul General for Germany in Scotland. This seminar provided the foundation for the present volume of essays that, although it does not claim to be comprehensive, offers an expert account of aspects of the history of the book in Germany over a period of some five hundred years.

The essays in this collection develop some of these themes in more detail. The volume opens with Mary Fischer's examination of the role played in the history of the book in Germany by the Knights of the Teutonic Order as a necessary concomitant to their twin objectives of military conquest of and spread of Christianity to Prussia. This is followed by Henrike Lähnemann's report of her research on a manuscript workshop in Stuttgart around 1475, which demonstrates the falsity of the widely held view that the late fifteenth century inaugurated the transformation of Europe to a print-based culture. John Flood moves the story firmly on to print with his close look at the typographical and authorial puzzles surrounding an imprint from 1479. In dealing with the sixteenth and early seventeenth centuries Jeffrey Ashcroft offers a perspective not dissimilar to Henrike Lähnemann in examining the acquisitions of St Andrews University Library during that period. The chronological advance of the volume moves to the seventeenth and eighteenth centuries with William Kelly's overview of scientific and medical publishing and another leap brings it up to the twentienth with Jasmin Adam's study of the role of advertising in the book trade and Alistair McCleery's exposure of the German origins of paperback publishing.

The Scottish Centre for the Book would like to thank Cate Newton, Brian Hillyard and Martyn Wade of the National Library of Scotland for their hospitality and support in the organization of the Seminar in May 2008. That Seminar would not have been possible also without the funding and moral support of the then German Consul General, Ingo Radcke, and his staff, particularly Beate Bidenbach, and our thanks are also due to them.

In opening the seminar, the Consul General stated: 'We Germans are intensely proud of being the nation that brought printing to the world. Like the Internet it revolutionised communications in Europe and then the world. The flood of pamphlets in German that marked the Reformation, and primarily Luther's translation of the Bible into German, helped to fix the German language and create a new sense of national identity. Fifty years after its appearance in Mainz, the printing press came to Edinburgh. Here too the printing press helped create a renewed sense of national identity and unity.' In publishing this book, we hope to repay some of the debt owed by all to the home of the printed word.

# Winning Hearts and Minds: the role of the written word in the Crusades in north-eastern Europe in the fourteenth century

*Mary Fischer*

The body of vernacular literature known as the *Deutschordensliteratur*, or 'the literature of the German Order' has been of lasting interest for researchers. None of the other major Orders has a comparable body of literature associated with it. It has been argued that the Order's leadership had a conscious policy of producing a body of devotional literature in the vernacular and may also have intended to produce a complete translation of the Bible into the vernacular in the first third of the fourteenth century. If so, this would place it at the forefront of systematic attempts to translate the Bible into German.

The idea that there was such a centrally controlled plan originated in the 1950s in the works of Karl Helm and Walther Ziesemer. They argued that the works belonged together on the basis of linguistic evidence, but also in terms of the themes and content, and that these were chosen to further the Order's priorities in Prussia:

> So ergibt sich das in der Ordensdichtung nur der Gedankenkreis des Ordens zur Geltung kam, in dessen Mittelpunkt der Orden selbst stand, und seine aus dem Kreuzzugsgedanken erwachsene religiös-kirchliche Aufgabe. Deshalb waren mit ganz geringen Ausnahmen nur zwei des Ordens würdige Stoffe behandelt: die Religion und die Ordensgeschichte.[1]

Helm and Ziesemer included in their *Deutschordensliteratur* some works which were demonstrably written by members of the Order along with others which appear to have been dedicated to the Order or have survived in manuscripts produced by the Order. They deduce from this that all of these works were written within the Order. Their claim that this represents a coherent, centrally planned process has been challenged by numerous researchers since and remains hotly debated. Interest in the topic has been given new impetus with the opening up of Eastern European libraries to western researchers and new attention has been given to the theory that the Order may have planned a complete Bible translation.[2]

What is remarkable about these works is first that such a large body of work exists, that it can be connected to the Order, either by authorship or by the manuscript tradition, and secondly the relatively short timescale within which they were produced. The Order did not produce any literature of this kind in the Holy Land, where it was founded in 1198 or during the early period in Prussia. The main period during which these works were written spans the period from about 1260 to 1340, with the greatest activity apparent between about 1300 and 1340.

The works known as the *Deutschordensliteratur* can be grouped into a series of loose categories. The earliest of these is a series of lives of saints. The earliest of the works considered part of the *Deutschordensliteratur* are the *Väterbuch* and the *Passional*.[3] The *Väterbuch* was written between 1265 and 1280. The author is unknown, but he is thought to have had links with the Order. It is based on the *Vitae Patrum* and is an account of the lives of the church fathers and saints and it ends with a depiction of the Last Judgement. The second major work is the *Passional*, which was written by the same author before the end of the thirteenth century. It is based largely on Jacob of Voragine's *Legenda Aurea*, a very colourful and popular account of lives of saints. In the 1290s two further popular works were written. In 1293 Hugo of Langenstein, a member of the Order, wrote a version of the legend of Saint Martina.[4] At around the same time Philipp of Seitz wrote a life of the Virgin Mary, which he notes in a postscript he has sent to the Order, obviously anticipating that it would be of interest to it. He dedicates the work to the Order:

> Auch ditz buechelin ich sende/Den bruodern von dem
> daeutschen haus/die han ih lange erkoern uz/Wand si gern
> marien erent/Und den glauben cristes merent.[5]

This suggests that contemporaries had noted the Order's interest in vernacular literature, and also that their cult of the Virgin, which became a feature of the Order's religious life in Prussia, was also known to contemporaries. The Order's full name was the Teutonic Order of St Mary's Hospital in Jerusalem and it made much of the significance of the Virgin as its patron in its later justification of its role in Prussia. The first five years of the fourteenth century saw the composition of a tract on morality *Der Sünden Widerstreit*, which is an allegorical, mystical poem about the conflict of virtue, under leadership of 'minne', or love, and evil, under the leadership of the devil.[6] In 1308 the later Grand Master of the Order, Luder of Brunswick, wrote the legend of Saint Barbara, which no longer survives and his chaplain, Nicolaus of Jeroschin, wrote a life of St Adalbert.[7] Both of these were missing from the *Passional* and both were important to the Order because of their links with Prussia and the Order. St Adalbert was the first Prussian martyr, having been killed during an attempt to convert the Prussians in 997. The relic of St Barbara's head is said to have been found in a church in Prussia in a context which resembles the finding of the Holy Lance in Jerusalem.[8]

The second category comprises a series of Bible translations. The first of these were translations of Judith and Esther, which date from the mid-thirteenth century. The author is unknown, but the texts survive only in manuscripts owned by the Order and it is possible they were written by priests in the Order.[9] The process accelerated at the beginning of the fourteenth century. Between 1300 and 1312 Heinrich von Hesler (1270-1347), wrote three works: an adaptation of the Apocalypse of St John, the Gospel of Nicodemus, an account of the four gospels which was very popular in the Middle Ages and a shorter poem called *Erlösung* (Salvation).[10] He also

Ill. 1:Above: *Prose Apocalypse*, fourteenth century: the Order fighting Gog & Magog.
Below: Heinrich von Hesler, *Apokalypse*, early fourteenth century
Toruń, Biblioteka Główna UMK, rkp 64 and rkp 44

devised an influential system of rhyme. A translation of the Books of the Maccabees was written between 1313 and 1322.[11] In 1331 Grand Master, Luder of Brunswick, commissioned a translation of Daniel.[12] In the same year *Von siben Ingesigeln* (Of seven seals), an account of the stages of Jesus' life, was written by Tilo of Kulm, who joined the Order in 1324 after a university education and a period as a cleric.[13] A paraphrase of the Book of Job was in existence by 1338 and the books of Ezra and Nehemiah were translated in the period between 1331 and 1340.[14] Finally a summary of the Old Testament was written under the title, *Historien der alden ê.*[15] (Ill. 1)

The third category of writing is historical. *The Livonian Rhymed Chronicle* was written by a knight in the Order, recording the conquest of Livonia, modern Latvia and Estonia, by the Sword Brothers and later the German Order.[16] Finally a chronicle of the Order's history in Prussia, the *Chronicon Terrae Prussiae*, was completed in 1326 by a priest in the Order, Peter of Dusburg, and was translated into German rhyme verse by the Order's chaplain, Nicolaus of Jeroschin.[17] (Ill. 2)

It cannot be a coincidence that the large majority of these works were produced in the first third of the fourteenth century. For some of the reasons why this might be it is necessary to look at the historical context in which the Order was operating. The military orders were founded in the Holy Land in response to the need of pilgrims for protection and for a permanent force to garrison the Holy Land. The first of the major orders to come into being was the Templars, who were founded in the aftermath of the First Crusade in 1096. They received their spiritual credentials from Bernard of Clairvaux's *De laude novae militiae*, written in 1129. He formalised the role of Christian warriors in the church as the *nova militia*, warriors whose role it was to follow Christ by pursuing their profession of bearing arms. The role of the new *militia Christi* was further formalised in the rule given to the Templars when they were officially endorsed by the Church in 1128/9. The Knights of St John were founded in 1099, while the German or Teutonic Order was founded by a group of German nobles a century later in 1198, after the Third Crusade. It was given the Rule of the Templars. It always had close links with the Hohenstaufen dynasty, and was skilful in exploiting these links to their advantage. In 1230 the Golden Bull issued by the Emperor Frederick II at Rimini, along with the bulls of Pope Gregory IX and an agreement with the Duke of Masovia, gave the Order free rein to conduct the crusade in Prussia. They were not to be subject to any secular overlord in this area, but only to the Pope, and as a result were able to build up a *de facto* overlordship over the areas they conquered. This meant that unlike the Templars and the Knights of St John, when the Christians lost Acre, their final outpost in the Holy Land, in 1291, the German Order still had an area in which they had papal sanction to carry on the crusade. The Order's headquarters were duly removed from the Holy Land to Venice in 1291 and to Prussia in 1309.

The consequences for the military orders as a whole for the loss of the Holy Land were severe. The Christians' failing fortunes in the East were

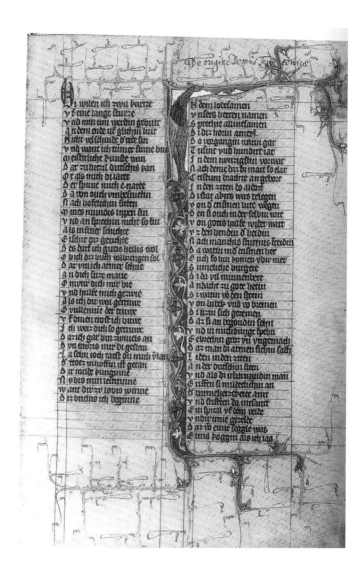

Ill. 2: Kronike von Pruzinlant: manuscript dating from the mid-fourteenth century. Stuttgart Landesbibliothek Cod. HB V 95 © Bildarchiv Foto Marburg

increasingly interpreted as a sign of God's displeasure with the whole venture. In the thirteenth century the Orders were accused, among other charges, of heresy, of neglecting the battle against the heathen and of exerting an authoritarian rule over the areas they controlled. This reaction culminated in the persecution of the Knights Templar from 1307, their disbandment in 1312 and the execution of many of its members, including the Grand Master, Jacques de Molay, in 1314.

The German Order's leadership must have been acutely aware of the necessity to avoid the fate of the Templars. To do so they had to defend themselves on several fronts. They had to convince the church and their contemporaries that their organisation was spiritually sound, that it was free of heresy and the practices of which the Templars had been accused, and was therefore a fit representative of Christendom in the war against the heathen. Without the backing of western Christendom the legitimacy of their crusade, their ability to attract crusaders and their entire raison d'être could be called into question.

In parallel to this, having completed the conquest of Prussia in 1293, the Order was increasingly engaged in running its own state, and in so doing it was having to confront the opposition of neighbouring and competing Christian powers. The Templars had been particularly unfortunate in having made an enemy of Philip IV of France, who was heavily in debt to them, but the German Order itself was by no means lacking in powerful enemies, largely as a result of its attempts to consolidate its position in Prussia. After being invited into Poland by the Duke of Łęczyca, later King Władysław I of Poland, to put down a rising on the Baltic coast, the Order seized and held on to Gdansk and the whole of Eastern Pomerania. This led to a dispute between the Order and Poland which continued throughout most of the fourteenth century. They were also in dispute with the Archbishop of Riga. War broke out with Riga in 1298. The Order was attempting to expand its influence in the area and came into conflict with the citizens of Riga, who in turn accepted the offer of a Lithuanian garrison to protect them. The Archbishop, Frederick of Riga, chose to support the citizens against the Order for his own purposes and accused the Order of preventing the clergy from preaching to the heathen and obstructing trade between Riga and Lithuania (which coincidentally was a pagan power, against whom the Order was leading crusades). The Archbishop also accused them of atrocities in 1310 and 1324. Pope Clement V instituted an enquiry into the complaints from Poland and Riga, found in Riga's favour in 1310 and excommunicated the Order. The excommunication was lifted in 1317.[18] This local opposition compounded the general difficulties which all the military orders were facing at this time.

However, ultimately all the orders stood or fell on whether they could justify their existence as the leaders of crusades. Internally this meant that their members had to be seen to be upholding their Rule. To the outside world it meant convincing contemporaries that they had the confidence of the church and that crusaders could redeem their crusading vows in the

Order's campaigns in North Eastern Europe. It is generally accepted that the Order embarked on a period of internal reform during the period under discussion in order to achieve these aims.[19]

By the end of the thirteenth century both the war in the Holy Land and the war in Prussia were over. The Order now had different, more wide ranging priorities. It still had to appeal to the nobility, in order to keep a steady supply of crusaders for the fourteenth century wars against the Lithuanians, but even more importantly it had to argue for and uphold its legitimacy within the church. It had to administer its newly secured territories, provide education, and enforce and uphold the Statutes. It had to maintain the Order's fundamental crusading ideology, deal with the Curia in Rome and enter into litigation with neighbouring powers. When the military orders were originally instituted, the lay knight brothers formed the leadership of the orders and the priest brothers occupied a more subservient role. There was no hierarchy among them and no provision for educating them.[20] However, in these new circumstances only the priest brothers had the learning necessary to undertake these roles and facilitate this process of adaptation. It is not surprising, therefore, that there appears to have been a rise in the status of the priesthood in the Order to coincide with all the events of the last years of the thirteenth and first years of the fourteenth century.

This rise in status of the priests and the increased emphasis on the spiritual needs of the knight brothers is shown symbolically in an illustration in a contemporary manuscript (Ill. 3). The illustration depicts a priest and knight brother in the Bible produced in 1321 for Luder of Brunswick, then Commander of Christburg. The Bible contained the two Books of the Maccabees and the New Testament. The initial below shows a knight and priest brother, both of whom are kneeling on either side of an open book, below a scene depicting the coronation of the Virgin. The book in which this appears is the prologue to the Books of the Maccabees, in which Luder of Brunswick is named as the patron of the work. The fact that the knight and the priest are shown as being of equal status suggests that this is not, as might be expected, a portrait of the patron, but is symbolic of the fact that knights and priests were now equally subject to the church and the scripture.[21]

Ill. 3 Krakow, Archivum Kapituty Metropolitanej Krakowskiej, Nr 63/10

Ill. 4. Initial from an Indulgence granted to a crusader in showing a member of the order, 1356, © Hessisches Staatsarchiv Marburg

Some of the clues about how the reform of the Order was carried out can be found in the additions to the Statutes at this time. Some of these new regulations relate to broad concerns, while others were obviously a response to the immediate emergency. One piece of evidence, for example, specifically suggests they were alert against the accusations of heresy and lewd behaviour levelled at the Templars. Of the few additional regulations enacted by the Grand Master, Burchard von Schwanden, in 1289, one focuses explicitly on ensuring that the charges of immoral behaviour which were being brought against the Templars were not laid at the German Order's door:

> Wir setzen von der brüdere cellen, daz die tûr wîte suln gegeterit sîn und mit nichte behangen, daz man wol darin muge gesehen, wer darinne sî.[22]

This regulation was repeated with increasing urgency three years later, in 1292 in the first and twelfth of the new regulations enacted by Conrad of Feuchtwangen:

> Wir wollen, daz man dekein bette behenge tages noch nahtes, sunder daz sie offenbar sîn, daz man wol ûf die bette muge sehen.[23]

However, beyond these specific responses to the needs of the moment there is also evidence of a broader, concerted effort to renew its sense of mission and its members' commitment to St Bernard's concept of the *militia Christi* and here too the regulations added to the Order's Statutes give an indication of the leaders' preoccupations. The Statutes enacted by Werner of Orseln, Grand Master from 1324 until 1330, focus on the observance of the church offices. Priests are to observe the offices 'more conscientiously than in the past' and provision is made for 'illiterate' knight brothers to say the Lord's Prayer, the Hail Mary and the Credo in German.[24]

There is also evidence that books were regarded as having an important part to play in this policy. In common with other religious orders, the original statutes of the order make provision for readings at mealtimes:

> Daruber sal man daz beholden in allen hûseren, dâ convent von brûderen ist, daz sint zwelf brûdere unde ein commendûr ....
> daz man da pflegelîche dî lectien zu tische habe, die alle die da ezzent, mit swîgene sullen hôren, daz in alleine di gûmen iht warden gespîset, sunder ouch ir ôren hungere nach gotes worte.[25]

There is evidence, again from later additions to the Statutes, that the acquisition of books was a matter of concern to the Order's officials. The *Gesetze über Meer*, dating from 1264 to 1289, specifically state that books left by brothers who had died were to be given to the Master of Germany to be disposed of according to his priorities. They also stipulate that any priest who has been given money to buy books must not use it for any other purpose without the express permission of the Master of Germany.[26] The regulation is repeated in 1289 immediately following Burchard von Schwanden's strictures on bedroom etiquette:

> Dekein brûder sol kein bûch von dem orden vremeden oder

vorkoufen âne urloup des gebieteres von dûtschen landen.[27]

For an Order which was predominately made up of fighting men, in which the priest brothers had traditionally and necessarily taken a subordinate role, the need for appropriate material to educate lay members of the Order in their calling in the new circumstances they faced at the beginning of the fourteenth century must have played a significant reason why the Order became known as a patron of literature at this time. The level of literacy, in the sense of being able to read Latin, in the Order in the thirteenth century is impossible to estimate. The earliest version of the rule states that many of the lay brothers were literate, but vernacular versions are less positive. It is however probable the knight brothers were literate in the sense of being able to read in the vernacular.[28] It is also likely that they were very familiar with the lay crusading epics which had become popular throughout the middle ages. Indeed, there is evidence for this in the text of the *Livonian Rhymed Chronicle*, which in its language, imagery and ideology is closer to one of these epics than to the *nova militia* proposed by Bernard of Clairvaux. It has already been noted that Hugo of Langenstein sent his life of the Virgin to the Order in the expectation that they would welcome it. There is evidence for the Order's preference for vernacular readings and that it was well known to contemporaries elsewhere, for example in a request in 1410 by nuns of the Clarissa Order in Nuremberg to have their readings in German, 'as is done here in the German Order'.[29]

The need for devotional literature in the vernacular to educate members is undoubtedly the reason for the impetus given at the beginning of the fourteenth century to the collection or commissioning of lives of saints and books of the Bible with which the Order has become associated. In fact there is speculation that the Order planned a complete translation of the Bible at this time. The final lines of the Books of the Maccabees, written around 1322, seem to indicate that a complete translation of the New Testament was planned for the future:

> Hie wirt dise rede Volant / daz die alde e ist irkant ( …)
> Machabaeorum genant. / die sullen sin die letzten bant ( ….)/
> So kumt die nuwe e gerant. /die sal man nemen vor die hant
> (…..) dar bringet uns die nuwe e / wand die alde entouc nicht
> me.[30]

Nonetheless, in this earlier period, when the Order is adjusting to its new role in Prussia and the new political situation in the first part of the fourteenth century, there is a marked and obvious preference for books of the Old Testament, such as Daniel, Judith, Esther and above all the Maccabees, who are models for the fight against the heathen and would appeal to the knights, and books such as Job, which teaches the correct attitude to adversity and setbacks. It is not until 1359 that the Marshal, Siegfried of Ragnit, commissioned Claus Cranc, a Franciscan, to translate the Prophets and another, unknown author translated the Acts of the Apostles that there is any further attempt to translate the Bible.[31]

While the need to look after the knight brothers' education was being taken care of through the translation of these books of the Bible and other works, the other pressing need, that of justifying the Order's role in Prussia to its members, the church and potential crusaders and supporters was met by the commissioning of yet another book, the *Chronicle of Prussia*.

The original version of this was written in Latin by Peter of Dusburg. It was commissioned by the Grand Master, Werner of Orseln, in 1326. Its purpose was threefold: it was a record of the Order's conquests in Prussia during the last century; it was a restatement of the military Order's original ethos; and it was a tool for justifying the Order's presence and activities in North Eastern Europe. The Latin text was a tool with which those charged with lobbying on the Order's behalf could find carefully argued theological and historical precedents and teleological justification of the Order's conquest of Prussia. However it was not best suited for the purpose of conveying the ideology to the bulk of the knight brothers who were unlikely to read the Latin.

Nicolaus of Jeroschin's translation, commissioned by the Grand Master, Luder of Brunswick, and written some time around 1340, served this purpose. It was his text which was most widely disseminated and later became the source for all accounts of the early history of Prussia. It was so successful that in fact Dusburg's original was lost and Jeroschin's version was translated back into Latin in the fifteenth century before the original was rediscovered in the seventeenth century.[32]

Little is known about Jeroschin as a man. He may have been born and brought up in Prussia. The dates of his life have generally been deduced from the text of the chronicle. He certainly reports events from around 1311 as an eye-witness and is likely to have been in Marienburg during the time the church there was renovated in the years leading up to 1344.

In his life of St Adalbert he describes himself as Chaplain to the Order in the service of Grand Master Luder of Brunswick, whose short period in office (1331-1335) coincided with a time in which many of the Bible translations were commissioned or acquired by the Order. The role of the Grand Master's chaplain was an influential one, and one of his roles was the supervision of the *Tischleser*, the officials who were responsible for the readings which took place at mealtimes. It seems certain, therefore, that Jeroschin played a pivotal role in the reform movement and in interpreting and implementing the Grand Master's policy. His motivation for translating the chronicle was, as he himself says, 'to make the work of the order more widely known in German speaking lands'.[33] His goal was to educate its lay members and beyond that, those noblemen who were not members, but whose support on crusade was necessary for the Order to function.

His intention is clear from the language, style and content of his version of Dusburg's chronicle. Jeroschin's chronicle is for the most part a translation of the original, but with significant changes in emphasis, tone and language. The content of the text is divided into an introduction and appeal to the

Holy Trinity, a short account of the origins of the Order in the Holy Land and a list of the Biblical prefigurations of the Order, including Abraham and Melchisedech, Moses and Joshua, King David and culminating in the Maccabees, with whom the Order most closely identified itself, discusses the role of the knights, which encompassed the tasks of fighting, providing hospitality and looking after the sick and of the priests, whose role was primarily that of encouraging the laymen to respect their rule and their calling.[34] The following section sets out a carefully argued justification of the wars, the use of arms in the service of Christian mission in a metaphorical but also in the literal sense. Based on St Paul's allegorical interpretation of Christian armour and the writings of Bernard of Clairvaux, this section sets up a justification of Christian warfare set firmly in the scholastic tradition, based on the writings of the Church Fathers and using Bible heroes as typological prefigurations of the knights.[35] The second part begins with the beginning of the war in Prussia, setting it carefully in the context of papal authority and noting the consent and agreement of the lay powers.[36] In the description of the wars he uses the language of the lay crusading epic, with which his audience would have been familiar; he emphasises the cult of the Virgin, as a counterpoint to the lay pursuit of courtly love and he intertwines references to local saints, in particular St Barbara and St Elizabeth, who were of particular interest to the Order. One of the most striking alterations he makes to Dusburg's version is the addition or expansion of sections which increase the 'human interest' of the story. He develops interesting anecdotes and includes emotive descriptions of the plight of the women who are captured by the heathen or descriptions of the celebrations of victories, one of the most striking of which is the account of the recovery of the relic of St Barbara.[37]

Finally how successful was this initiative? One measure of its success is that the Order survived a full century until the conclusive defeat at Grunwald (Tannenberg) in 1410. During the fourteenth century its crusades against Lithuania became the medieval equivalent of the Grand Tour for western European knighthood (Ill. 4). Chaucer's knight included Prussia and Russia among the scenes of his triumphs.[38] The Order's territory even became the scene of early Anglo-Scottish antagonism in a famous incident in which a Scottish knight, taking a break from killing the English after the battle of Otterburn, is killed in a skirmish between the Scots and the English on a bridge in Königsberg in 1391.[39]

The Order achieved this status, ironically, by restating and reinvigorating an obsolescent eleventh and twelfth century ideology in a more extreme form in their chronicles. They were also able to exploit and harness the beginnings of a more modern approach to spirituality, represented by an increased desire among the population as a whole for access to the Scriptures and devotional writing in the vernacular. The authors whose works they collected or commissioned contributed to the development of a vernacular tradition of Bible texts of very high quality. It has been demonstrated that the works of Claus Cranc show a vitality and modernity of language which is only achieved again in Luther's translation, nearly two hundred years later. By providing the conditions in which Bible translations could be written, studied and disseminated, paradoxically, in trying to strengthen church doctrine, they were also paradoxically unintentionally instrumental in fostering the conditions which ultimately led to the overthrow of Church authority.

## Notes

1 Karl Helm and Walther Ziesemer, *Die Literatur des Deutschen Ritterordens* (Giessen: Wilhelm Schmitz Verlag, 1951), p. 41 and p.120. 'The result was that only themes related to the Order's ideology were represented in its literature, and at its centre was the Order itself and its religious and ecclesiastical task, rooted in the ideology of the crusades.'

2 Jelko Peters, 'Zum Begriff *Deutschordensdichtung*: Geschichte und Kritik', *Berichte und Forschungen*, 3 (1995), 7-38; Arno Mentzel Reuters, *Arma Spiritualia: Bibliotheken, Bücher und Bildung im Deutschen Orden* (Wiesbaden: Harrassowitz Verlag, 2003) (Beiträge zum Buch- und Bibliothekswesen 47), 31; Freimut Löser, 'Auf dem Weg zur deutschen Bibel. Prosaübersetzungen des Neuen Testaments aus dem Deutschen Orden', in Bernhart Jähnig, ed. *Kirchengeschichtliche Probleme des Preussenlandes aus Mittelalter und Früher Neuzeit* (Marburg: N.G. Elwert Verlag, 2001), 163-198 (189).

3 *Das Väterbuch*, ed. Karl Reissenberger, Deutsche Texte des Mittelalters XXII (Berlin, 1914); *Das Passional. Eine Legendensammlung des 13. Jahrhunderts,* ed. Fr. K. Köpke, (Quedlinburg: Basse, 1852) (Bibliothek der National-Literatur, 32).

4 Hugo of Langenstein, *Legende der heiligen Martina*, ed. Adelbert von Keller, (Stuttgart: 1856) (Bibliothek des literarischen Vereins in Stuttgart, 38).

5 'I am sending this book to the brothers of the German House, as has been my intention for some time, because they are great devotees of the Virgin Mary and are spreading the Christian faith.' Kurt Gärtner, Bruder Philipp, OCart, in VL vol 7, 588-597, here 593f.

6 *Der Sünden Widerstreit. Eine geistliche Dichtung des 12. Jahrhunderts,* ed. V Zeidler (Graz, 1892).

7 *Das Leben des heiligen Adalbert,* ed. Ernst Strehlke, Scriptores Rerum Prussicarum II (Leipzig: Hirzel, 1861 -), pp. 423-428

8 Nicolaus von Jeroschin, *Die Kronike von Pruzinlant,* ed. Ernst Strehlke, Scriptores Rerum Prussicarum I (Leipzig: Hirzel, 1861), pp. 303-624, lines 6277-6670.

9 Manfred Caliebe, *Hester. Eine poetische Paraphrase des Buches Esther aus dem Ordensland Preußen.* Edition und Kommentar, Quellen und Studien zur Geschichte des Deutschen Ordens, 21 (Marburg: N. G. Elwert, c1985); Peters, *Deutschordensdichtung* (note 2), p. 26f.;

Henrike Lähnemann, *Hystoria Judith: Deutsche Judithdichtung vom 12. bis zum 16. Jahrhundert* (Berlin: Walther de Gruyter, 2006), pp.189-298.

10  Heinrich von Hesler, *Apokalypse. Aus der Danziger Handschrift*, ed. Karl Helm, Deutsche Texte des Mittelalters VIII (Hildesheim: Weidmann, 2005); *Das Evangelium Nicodemi von Heinrich von Hesler*, ed. Karl Helm (Hildesheim: Olms, 1976); *Erlösung*, ed. Heinemann and E Steinmeyer, *Zeitschrift für deutsches Altertum 32* (1888) pp.110-117.

11  *Das Buch der Maccabäer*, ed. Karl Helm, (Tübingen: gedruckt für den literarischen Verein in Stuttgart, 1904) (Bibliothek des Literarischen Vereins in Stuttgart 233).

12  *Daniel: eine Deutschordensdichtung*, ed. Arthur Hübner (Berlin: Mayer & Müller, 1911).

13  Tilo von Kulm, *Von siben Ingesigeln*, ed. Karl Kochendörffer (Berlin: Weidmann, 1907).

14  Theodor E. Karsten, ed., *Die mitteldeutsche poetische Paraphrase des Buches Hiob*, (Berlin: 1910) (Deutsche Texte des Mittelalters, 21); *Esdras und Neemyas: eine Deutschordensdichtung aus dem 14. Jahrhundert*, ed. S. D. Stirk, Sprache und Kultur der germanischen und romanischen Völker, IV (Breslau: Priebatsch, 1938).

15  *Historien der alden ê*, ed. Wilhelm Gerhard (Leipzig: K. W. Hiersemann, 1927) (Bibliothek des Literarischen Vereins in Stuttgart 271).

16  *Livländische Reimchronik*, ed. Leo Meyer (Hildesheim: G. Olms, 1963, reprint of the 1876 Paderborn edition).

17  Peter von Dusburg, *Chronicon terrae Prussiae*, Scriptores Rerum Prussicarum I (Leipzig: Hirzel, 1861; reprinted Frankfurt am Main, 1965) pp3-219; *Peter von Dusburgs Chronik des Preußenlandes*, translated and edited by Klaus Scholz and Dieter Wojtecki (Darmstadt: Wissenschaftliche Buchgesellschaft, 1984); Nicolaus of Jeroschin, *Kronike von Pruzinlant*, see note 8.

18  S. C. Rowell, *Lithuania Ascending: a pagan empire within east-central Europe, 1295-1345* (Cambridge: Cambridge University Press, 1994) pp. 14-15.

19  Arno Mentzel-Reuters, *Arma Spiritualia* (Wiesbaden: Harrassowitz Verlag, 2003) pp. 22-28.

20  Ibid., p. 25.

21  Ibid., p.27; Jerzy Domasłowski, 'Malerei in Deutschordensland Preußen', in Udo Arnold, ed., *Deutscher Orden 1190-1990* (Lüneburg: Institut für Nordostdeutsches Kulturwerk,1997) (Tagungsberichte der historischen Kommission für Ost- und Westpreussische Landesforschung 11) pp.131-170

22  *Die Statuten des Deutschen Ordens nach den ältesten Handschriften*, ed., Max Perlbach (Halle: Max Niemeyer, 1890), p.139, l. 25-26. 'We decree that there should be no hangings round the beds, either during the day or at night, but that they should be open so that the beds can

be clearly seen.'

23 *Statuten*, p.140, l. 24-25

24 Ibid., p. 147, l. 22-24.

25 Ibid., p. 41, l. 17f. 'In all houses in which there is a full complement of twelve brothers and a commander ... it should be the rule that readings are held at mealtimes, and all those who are eating should listen in silence, so that not only their physical needs are nourished, but their hunger for the word of God.'

26 Ibid., p. 135, l. 6-14.

27 Ibid., p. 139, l. 29-32. 'No brother may sell or otherwise remove any book from the Order without the permission of the Master of Germany.'

28 Alan Forey, 'Literacy and learning in the Military Orders during the twelfth and thirteenth centuries', in Helen Nicholson, ed., *The Military Orders, vol. 2, Welfare and Warfare* (Aldershot: Ashgate, 1998), pp. 185-206, p. 186.

29 Quoted in Arno Mentzel-Reuters, pp 76-77.

30 *Das Buch der Maccabäer*, p. 400-401, lines 14231-14280: 'This marks the end of the section known as the Books of the Maccabees in the Old Testament. Now it is the turn of the New Testament to be taken in hand. Bring the New Testament because the Old Testament is no longer enough.'

31 Löser, pp. 172-179.

32 Udo Arnold and Lotte Kurras, 'Nikolaus von Jeroschin: Kronike von Pruzinlant', in *800 Jahre Deutscher Orden. Ausstellungskatalog des Germanischen Nationalmuseums*, ed. Gerhart Bott and Udo Arnold (Gütersloh/München: Bertelsmann Lexikon Verlag,1990), pp.97-98.

33 *Kronike von Pruzinlant*, l. 160-165.

34 Ibid., l. 835-890.

35 Ibid, l. 855-864, l. 2130-3390.

36 Ibid., l. 1498ff.

37 Ibid., l. 6365- 6670.

38 *The Riverside Chaucer*, ed. Larry D. Benson (Oxford: 1988), p.24, lines 53-55.

39 Werner Paravicini, *Die Preussenreisen des Europäischen Adels* (Sigmaringen: Jan Thorbecke Verlag, 1989), pp.135-138; Alan MacQuarrie, *Scotland and the Crusades 1095-1560* (Edinburgh: John Donald, 1997), pp.85-86.

# From Print to Manuscript: the case of a manuscript workshop in Stuttgart around 1475

*Henrike Lähnemann*

As part of a larger project on late medieval German manuscripts Heidelberg University Library has recently digitised a group of manuscripts under the name of "Werkstatt des Ludwig Henfflin".[1] As the initiators of the project point out, this is a special case among the many treasures of the library because, as far as we know, these nine manuscripts form a distinct group that has been kept together since its production around 1475 in the Stuttgart area for Margaret of Savoy, then Duchess of Württemberg.[2] Between 1453 and her death in 1479 she lived in Stuttgart as the third wife of Ulrich V of Württemberg, and it was here at the end of her life that she must have commissioned the group of manuscripts. After her death the nine manuscripts, one still unfinished and all probably still unbound, went to Heidelberg where the Elector Palatine Philip, Margaret's son from a previous marriage, incorporated them in his library.

The group is named after a scribal entry in the heroic epic, Sigenot: *Hie haut rys Sigenot ein end/ Got vns allen kummer wend/ Ludwig Henfflin* (Here ends the story about the giant Sigenot. May God preserve us from all trouble). It can be assumed that this Ludwig Henfflin was a main figure in the workshop which employed several scribes and beside one main illuminator several collaborators of different skills and patience. No archival record has been found to substantiate the workshop hypothesis and it might have been an *ad hoc* formation for this particular order by the duchess. The only indication of a date given in the manuscripts is the figure, 1477, written on the steps of the throne of King Saul in the second volume of the three-volume Old Testament.[3]

The "Henfflin Workshop" as a unity is determined by paper with the same watermarks, by "Zeichner A", the illuminator who was responsible for most of the drawings throughout the manuscripts with the exception of Cpg 76, and by recurring scribal hands.[4]

Cpg 16–18  Old Testament
Cpg 67     'Sigenot'
Cpg 76     'Ackermann von Böhmen'
Cpg 142    'Pontus und Sidonia'
Cpg 152    'Historie von Herzog Herpin'
Cpg 345    'Lohengrin' and 'Friedrich von Schwaben'
Cpg 353    'Die Heidin'

The group of manuscripts allows a unique insight into the production of illuminated manuscripts subsequent to the establishment of printing in the Southern German speaking area.[5] From the standpoint of literary history the mixture of texts may appear random. There seems no unifying feature apart from all of them being in German and all of them being illuminated. Next to the highly rhetorical contemporary prose work 'Ackermann von Böhmen' stands the heroic verse epic 'Sigenot', one of the later adventures of Dietrich of Bern and one of the early bestsellers of printing history. There are translations of scandal novels from French such as the 'Herpin', the adventure story of 'Pontus und Sidonia', also translated from French, and 'Lohengrin', a courtly romance. Cpg 16–18, a full set of the Books from the Old Testament, is copied from the German Bible printed by Mentelin in Strasbourg around 1466.[6] The key to understanding the manuscripts and the choice of the topics lies, I would claim, not in the text side but in the wishes of the patroness for a certain type of book: the illuminated vernacular manuscript as an object for representational entertainment, an element missing from the newly emerging formats of the printing press. The activity of the "workshop" is to pursue her ideal of a courtly library when revising the texts, developing the layout for the different genres and devising the iconography.

By way of introduction I shall therefore give a brief overview on the bibliophile background of Margaret before analysing those texts where printed editions exist, whether as a direct model or as contemporary parallels.

## Margaret of Savoy as patroness

The eventful life of its patroness, Margaret of Savoy, spans the turbulent century from a courtly upbringing in the French-speaking realm to an established literary community in southwest Germany, one generation after the introduction of the printing press. In the manuscript production of the Henfflin Workshop the socio-cultural setting of a courtly culture meets the modern book market. The printing network influenced what texts could be obtained for copying, what training was available for scribes and literary agents and what models for text-image relationship were prevalent. The commission of tailor-made manuscripts for Margaret drew on a wide selection of texts that also allowed the patroness to show off in different ways.

One way was the integration of her coat of arms in various forms. A forthright representational setting (which was continued in printed books in the form of book plates) can be found in an elaborate drawing on the opening page of the 'Ackermann von Böhmen', where the coat of arms is shown in the form of two shields done in trompe-l'œil fashion, each hung on an imaginary peg, casting shadows on the wall represented by the page. [Ill. 1] On the left shield, i.e. the heraldic prominent right hand side, are the three antlers of Württemberg; on the other side, reserved for the female line, the white cross of Savoy on a red field, later to become the Swiss flag, is shown. The same arms of alliance recur twice as a bas-de-page drawing in 'Friedrich von Schwaben' where the name of the protagonist seems to have triggered the showing of the Swabian alliance with Savoy, especially the second time where it appears next to the lines talking about Friedrich of Swabia's son inheriting his mother's country: *ward im gegeben / Siner muter land gantz eben* (ll. 8059f).[7] [Ill. 2] The Savoy coat of arms on its own with its very basic structure which allowed it to be downscaled to miniature size pops up through all the illustrations: as bas-de-page decoration in drawn-out curves of letters of the top- or bottom-line of writing. Sometimes it is combined with the device *fortuna* but, more hidden, as part of the illumination, for example, the red flag with the white cross flies over the tent of the Christian hero preparing for a tournament with the Saracens in 'Die Heidin', an epic adventure.[8] [Ill. 3]

The importance of this courtly identity device can also be seen on two panels from the 1460s, formerly part of a triptych.[9] Ulrich V, "the much loved", also called *Gotznieswurtz* after his favourite curse, on the left is kneeling opposite his three wives on the right, all of them daughters of counts, with their coats of arms: Margaret of Cleve (+1444), Elisabeth of Bavaria-Landshut (+1451) and Margaret of Savoy (+1479) with the silver cross on the red ground.[10] Margaret of Savoy thus is shown between the coats of arms that were then painted in the manuscripts.

It was also the third marriage of Margaret of Savoy (*1420). After growing up as the youngest daughter of Count Amadeus VIII of Savoy and his wife, Marie of Burgundy, in a literary rich tradition, she had been married in absentia to Louis III of Anjou, titular king of Sicily (*1403 +1434), who was in Italy fighting for his dominion.[11] When, after three years of nominal marriage, she went to meet him, the news of his sudden death reached her in Cosenza. At least she retained the title of a queen, and was celebrated by the French court poets of the day, especially in the 'Champion des dames', written by her father's clerk, Martin LeFranc, in 1440:

> Mais d'une diray entre mille
> Laquelle porte le vesvage
> Pour le roy Loys de Cecile
> Que Mort ravi en trop vert age
> C'est une reyne belle et sage
> Tant de vertu enluminee
> Qu'elle est a tout humain visage
> Comme la clere matinee.

> (But I will talk about one among a thousand, one who wears widow's weeds for the King Louis of Sicily whom death stole away at a much too tender age. She is a beautiful and wise queen, so much illuminated by virtue that she is for all humans to behold like the bright morning.)

> Pour les grans biens qui sont en elle,
> Souvent l'ay voulu haultement

Loer de loenge nouvelle,
Mais onq n'y avins justement.
Neantmains en son nom proprement,
**Marguerite de Savoye,**
Vous trouverez tout rondement:
**Vertu me garde sa joye.**[12]
(Because of the great goodness that is in her, I have often intended
to laud her highly with renewed praise, but I could not do this
adequately. However in her proper name "Margaret of Savoy" you
find it all nicely rounded [i.e. anagrammatically turned] as "Virtue
guards for me its joy".)

This was the type of literature with which Margaret was familiar:
exceedingly rhetorical French romance, illustrated to a high standard, as
can be seen by the French manuscripts in the Palatine Library which were
probably brought by her to Heidelberg.[13] In 1444 she married Ludwig
IV, Elector Palatine (*1424, +1449) and moved to Heidelberg. To the
French historiographers this seemed a steep decline but, in fact, she was
still in a Francophile sphere: her mother-in-law was a distant relative from
another branch of the Savoy family and many of her peers, the noble
women married to the dukes and counts of Southern Germany, came from
French speaking areas and acted as translators: Eleanor of Austria (*1433
in Scotland, raised at the French court, +1480) is acclaimed as translator
of the prose novel, 'Pontus und Sidonia', in the first print [Ill. 4]; Elizabeth
of Nassau-Saarbrücken (*1394 in Nancy, + 1456) translated the French
novels, 'Loher und Maller', 'Huge Scheppel', 'Herpin' and 'Sibille' of
which the 'Herpin' later was to form part of the commission by Margaret
of Savoy.

This gives an idea of what Margaret was looking for when she
commissioned the manuscripts after moving to Stuttgart to marry Ulrich
V in 1453: vernacular stories in the form of illuminated manuscripts,
noble entertainment finished to a high standard. She had to leave all her
books behind in Heidelberg and had to start from scratch in recreating
a noblewoman's library. Since the manuscripts are fairly homogenous in
appearance and share the same paper, they were probably commissioned
as a group only in the late 1470s, around the date 1477 given in the
Old Testament. The group seems to have been unfinished still at the
time of Margaret's death in 1479 when the manuscripts were probably
left unbound, since some of the pages came to be bound with other
manuscripts, and the rubrics in the Ackermann-manuscript were missing.

### The "Henfflin Workshop"
Margaret's expectation from the Henfflin Workshop determined how they
set to work. None of the works they executed was at that time available
in the form of an illuminated manuscript which they could have copied

Ill. 1: Heidelberg University Library, Cpg 76, f. 1ᵛ (Ackermann von Böhmen): Coat of Arms of Margaret of Savoy as Duchess of Württemberg-Urach
© Universitätsbibliothek Heidelberg

Ill. 2: Heidelberg University Library, Cpg 345, f. 379ʳ (Friedrich von Schwaben): Coat of Arms of Margaret of Savoy as Duchess of Württemberg-Urach
© Universitätsbibliothek Heidelberg

Ill. 3: Heidelberg University Library, Cpg 353, f. 6ᵛ (Die Heidin): Savoy flag flying on the tent of Wittige of Jordan
© Universitätsbibliothek Heidelberg

directly, except for the Old Testament – actually the work that might have inspired Margaret since she could see from her late husband's copy that German workshops were capable of illuminating manuscripts, though in a very different style from what she was used to from her youth. But that was not available to borrow, so for each of the texts the workshop had to find an individual solution. However, the Lauber Workshop that was active a generation earlier in Alsace provides a good point of comparison since it is the earliest known workshop to produce a large number of illuminated German manuscripts.[14] These workshop products from Alsace can be distinguished from the form of illuminated manuscripts Margaret was familiar with from her youth in Savoy by the fact that they were not costly singular pieces on parchment adorned with gold and the coat of arms of the patron.[15]

Ill. 4 Pontus und Sidonia-Print: Bayerische Staatsbibliothek München 2 Inc.c.a. 3649 (Pontus und Sidonia, Augsburg: Johann Schönsperger, 1498, f. a2ʳ)

The Lauber Workshop streamlined the production of manuscripts, writing only on paper, with drawings that could be coloured in with a restricted palette. Some of them were even produced in advance for prospective buyers, for example popular texts such as Wolfram of Eschenbach's 'Parzival'. These clients could still be the high nobility, as the example of the Palatine court shows, but even more often they were prosperous merchants in those towns that were to become hubs of the printing industry which could take over distribution strategies and clientele from the Lauber Workshop.

The Henfflin manuscripts present a union of the manuscript manufacture tradition in the German speaking area and the courtly idea of the commissioned elaborate artefact. What the Lauber Workshop produces for Margaret of Savoy are the stock-in-trade vernacular texts of the late fifteenth century, on paper without gold and expensive colours, but they are also individual pieces for most of the time the only illuminated manuscript copy of the text. In addition the illustrations are pencil-washed drawings but staged as illuminations: framed, with detailed background and specifically designed captions. Each of the manuscripts had been through a process of careful editing, either through text adaptations or by iconographic new devices, quite often both of them. I shall concentrate on three examples where contemporary prints allow a comparison of the style, status and layout of the texts.

### Cpg 16–18: The Old Testament

The Old Testament was directly copied from a print, the German Bible, printed before 1466 by Mentelin.[16] He used a much smaller type than Gutenberg, which allowed him to accommodate more text on the pages and he included no illustrations. What the workshop did to turn this material into an illuminated manuscript is repeated in the other volumes, a fact which points to an overall editor for this, possibly the Ludwig Henfflin who writes the *subscriptio* in the Sigenot-volume: breaking up the text into convenient portions and devising captions which were written in red above the frame that marked places for the illustrations that were to be executed. An intriguing insight in the close collaboration between the scribe / editor and the illuminator can be seen in one of the miniatures for the Book of Judith. [Ill. 5]

Ill. 5: Heidelberg University Library, Cpg 17, f. 255ᵛ (Judith hands Holofernes' head over to her maid) © Universitätsbibliothek Heidelberg

### Wie Judith Holiferns sin houbt abschnait als er lag an sinem bette (Cpg 17, f. 255v)[17]

Jdt 13, 8 Vnd da sy dis hatt gesagt sy genahet sich zů dem haubt sins bettes vnd lost vff sin swert das da hing an ir. 9 Vnd da sy es hatt ußgezogen sy begraiff das har sins houbts vnd sprach O herre got israhel sterck mich zů der stund. 10 Vnd sy slůg zwir in sin halsaderen vnd schnaid ab sin houbt (255vb) vnd nam ab sin küssy von den sülen vnd welczet ab sinen lib den stamm. 11 Vnd darnach ain lützel ging sy uß vnd antwurt holofernis houbt irer dirn vnd gebot das sy es legt in ir tasche. 12 Vnd sy gingen baid uß nach ir gewonhait als zů dem gebet vnd fürgingen die herbergen vnd vmbgingen das tal...

### How Judith cut off Holofernes' head while he was lying on his bed[18]

Jdt 13,8 and when she had said that, she drew near to the head of his bed and untied the sword that was hanging at it. 9 And when she had unsheathed it, she gripped the hair of his head and said: "O Lord God Israel, strengthen me in this hour." 10 And she slashed his jugular veins twice and cut off his head and took down his pillow from the column and pushed down his body, the trunk. 11 And shortly after that, she went out and passed the head of Holofernes to her maid and ordered her to put it in the bag. 12 And both of them went out as they were wont to do for prayer and passed the tents and went round the valley...

The caption for the culminating moment in the Book of Judith is independent from the Bible text that gives the gory procedure in long-winded sentences typical of the literal translation of the 14th century that formed the basis for the text of the Mentelin Bible. But the illumination does not show the action described in the caption, Judith in the act of cutting off Holofernes' head, but rather the immediately following scene: The torso of Holofernes is left behind in the tent and Judith hands his severed head to her maid while they both hold a curious looking pouch; it has the same pattern as the pillow case in Holofernes' tent. This arises from how the translator of this bible version rendered the *conopeum* for the trophy Judith takes from Holofernes' tent to show later to the citizens of Betulia (Jdt 13,10 *et percussit bis in cervicem eius et abscidit caput eius et abstulit conopeum eius a columnis et evolvit corpus eius truncum*).[19] In antique literature it meant a mosquito net but since it is a hapax legomenon in the Bible, none of the translators of the 14th century was sure what it meant; the first branch translated it as *umbhank* (coat) and the twelfth branch kept the word as a loan word *conopeum*.[20] The second branch on which the

Mentelin Bible and eventually the Henfflin manuscript was based tried to hit the meaning with *küssy* ("cushion") and identified this object with the bag used to transport the head (Jdt 13,11 *iussit ut mitteret illud in peram suam*). This unique feature of Holofernes' head in a chequered pillowcase proves that the illuminator must have been familiar with the text as it stands in the manuscript and that rather than resorting to standard devices, he carefully showed as many of the actual details as possible, like the crowd of listless Assyrian soldiers squeezed into the image by reducing them to the round back of their helmet (approximately fifty silvery blots).

What has been observed from this page could be repeated for many of the other pictures: even iconic iconography is enhanced and elaborated by close attention to the actual text. At the same time, the illustrations are much more numerous than in the contemporary parallels. While the Lauber manuscript of the Bible has just one image per biblical book, in the Henfflin Old Testament the Book of Judith (f. 245r–259r) alone has ten images, placed at dramatic moments of the story. The illustrations start with only one image for chapter six (f. 248v: Achior is bound to a tree) and chapter seven (f. 249v: Holofernes starts the siege of Betulia) and then focuses completely on Judith's story. After leaving Bethulia (f. 252v) and being presented to Holofernes (f. 253v), the narrative unfolds blow by blow, page by page, with four illustrations for chapter thirteen alone: The meal with Holofernes (f. 255r), the head being put in the bag (f. 255v), returning to the city (f. 256r) and showing the proofs to the city council (f. 256v) [Ill. 6].

Ill. 6: Heidelberg University Library, Cpg 17, f. 256v (Judith shows the head of Holofernes while her maid presents the pillow case)
© Universitätsbibliothek Heidelberg

Since one of the proofs is the *conopeum* (Jdt 13,19 *Ecce caput Holoférnis príncipis milítiæ Assyriórum, et ecce conópeum illíus, in quo recumbébat in ebrietáte sua*), the illustration faithfully repeats the pillow case scenario, the blue-and-white chequered material decorated with a large blood stain; the exact rendering, again, required reading not only the caption that mentions the *küssy* just as an object but the full text that explains that this is actually the pillow on which Holofernes was resting and which therefore has to be blood-stained.

The last two illustrations show again the action from Judith's viewpoint: she sets the flight of the Assyrian army into motion by holding Holofernes' head over the town walls (f. 257v) and on the opposite side (f. 258r) she continues watching from this post when the Israelites set upon the disheartened army.[21] By this form of teichoscopy Judith emerges quasi as the narrator of the picture cycle. This ties in with the strict concentration on the historical meaning of the Bible: throughout the poetic books there is not a single illustration to be found which had the effect that the first illumination in the third volume of the Old Testament (Cpg 18) only comes on f. 255r, showing Ezekiel in action. Whenever it is possible in this pictorial retelling of the history of the Old Testament, noblewomen are fore grounded and shown in the latest fashion, regardless whether they are Pharaoh's daughter, Judith or the Queen of Sheba.

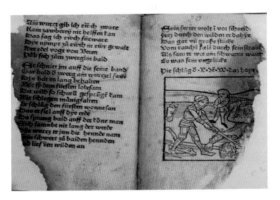

Ill. 7: Sigenot Print: Germanisches Nationalmuseum Nürnberg, 8° Inc. 114115 (Augsburg: Johann Bämler, ca. 1487, f. C1v/C2r).

### The Sigenot manuscript

The special feature of the illustration of the Old Testament, namely that the images form fully fledged narrative cycles, has been taken to extremes in the Sigenot manuscript.[22] There were no precedents for illustrating German heroic epic; while other secular genres (Arthurian romances, Love Lyrics) had slowly started to be represented in illuminated manuscripts over the thirteenth and fourteenth century, texts like the 'Nibelungenlied' and the heroic epic surrounding Dietrich of Bern had been confined to unspectacular manuscripts, decorated if at all only with ornamental initials. Therefore the first task confronting the editor was the division of the text to define the places for the illustrator. The contemporary printers, who started around the same time in Augsburg to print the first edition of Sigenot which was rapidly followed by numerous reprints, interspersed the narrative in more or less regular intervals with woodcuts. [Ill. 7] Johann Bämler positioned all woodcuts with their captions at the bottom of the octave sized pages which were laid out for twenty five lines of text; this meant that the woodcuts and their captions would inevitably cut through one of the thirteen-lined verses.[23]

The Henfflin editor apparently wanted to avoid this splitting up of verses. Instead, he opted for taking each verse as a separate unit to be illustrated. [Ill. 8] This resulted in a very peculiar lay-out which never was repeated, neither for the 'Sigenot' nor any other heroic epic: each of the 201 pages is divided between a framed image on the top half and a thirteen-line verse on the bottom half. Since large portions of the text consist of dialogues or duels, easily drawn out over a dozen verses, the effect is similar to looking at film stills in slow motion.

Ill. 8 Sigenot Manuscript, Heidelberg University Library, Cpg 67, f. 21ᵛ/22ʳ © Universitätsbibliothek Heidelberg

### The 'Pontus und Sidonia' manuscript

By choosing the prose novel 'Pontus und Sidonia' to be turned into an illuminated manuscript, the Henfflin Workshop picked again, as with the 'Sigenot', a text that became one of the early bestsellers of the German printing industry.[24] In this case the solutions for distributing the images in the narrative are parallel, though not identical, since the prose text allowed placing the illustrations at the most convenient point. But the effect achieved by this is quite different. In the manuscript, the first miniature comes only when a significant action takes place, after two pages of text. [Ill. 4] By contrast, the first woodcut in the print-edition by Schönsperger is prominently placed on the first page, together with a blurb: a print has to sell its contents to a prospective buyer and therefore the title-page is developed, a form of lay-out superfluous for a manuscript where the patron or patroness knows exactly what she commissioned and why.[25] [Ill. 9]

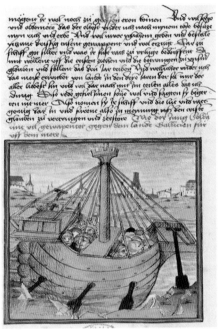

Ill. 9 Pontus und Sidonia Ms., Heidelberg University Library, Cpg 142, f. 1ᵛ: The Sultan sets sail to attack Gallicia. © Universitätsbibliothek Heidelberg

To conclude: by turning "from manuscript to print" on its head I wanted to counteract the implicit teleology of the well-worn phrase, the popular misunderstandings of manuscripts and prints as stages in the development of literacy. In certain areas manuscript production was not extinguished by the printing press but rather encouraged and diversified. A very considerable number of seminal manuscripts for what we think of as medieval German literature were produced at a time when it would have been just as easy to have it printed; without the 'Ambraser Heldenbuch', the manuscript collection of novels and heroic epic commissioned by Emperor Maximilian, we would not have the full text of the earliest German Arthurian novel, the 'Erec'.[26]

The Henfflin Workshop rose to the challenge of its noble patroness by re-inventing the idea of the illuminated vernacular manuscript. Manuscripts keep up the idea of vernacular literature as courtly entertainment in the age of printing and opening up of text production to a much wider audience. The workshop developed a specific style of formalized illustration and layout that held together the group of manuscripts despite the variety of its genres and sources and turned it into a distinct noble set of texts. This feature was seen by the early publications on the Palatine library as a lack of originality and individuality. Wegener writes in his catalogue of the illuminated manuscripts of the Heidelberg University Library in 1927:

> Die Arbeit ist sorgfältig, aber sehr temperament- und phantasielos ... Die übertriebene Eleganz der Figuren in Kleidung und Geste, die affektlose Ruhe der Bilder, die starke Vertiefung und Ausschmückung der Bildbühne, die allerdings durch primitive Mittel zu erreichen versucht ist, zeigen deutlich, daß der Zeichner von dem Wunsch der Bestellerin nach einer höfischen Illustrationsform stark beeinflußt ist. Der Qualität des Zeichners entsprechend ist das Resultat seiner Bemühungen unbedeutend. Für eine steife und leere Eleganz gibt er alle volkstümliche Kraft auf.[27]
>
> (The work has been done diligently but without temperament and imagination ... The overdone elegance of the figures' attire and gesture, the emotion-drained immobility of the images, the great depth and decoration of the imaginary stage which however has been tried to achieve by primitive means – they all show that the illustrator has been strongly influenced by the patroness' wish for a courtly form of illumination. In accordance with the quality of the illustrator the result of his endeavours is meagre. He sacrifices all home-grown, natural strength to achieve a stiff and empty elegance.)

Later voices have found more positive words. In her introduction to the facsimile of the 'Herpin' manuscript Ute von Bloh has characterized the work of the Henfflin workshop as an independent and inventive way to cast courtly models in the mould of contemporary manuscripts.[28] This is not only true for the 'Herpin' but can be read as a description of the editing efforts of this group of scribes and illustrators: finding a viable balance between representation and usage, of combining recognisable schemes of illustration (for example the recurrent scenes of parting) with the minutiae of the individual text and its detailed descriptions.

Illumination had always been a mark of distinction not only for the patron, whose wealth was a perquisite for it, but more for certain types of book: theological and historical subjects, predominately Latin. Until printing made heroic epics easily available, even though one might squirm at the term "Volksbuch", an illuminated heroic epic was a contradiction in itself. Manuscript production in the age of printing gives the manuscripts and its patrons a new status. The tailor-made erudite application of forms of representation until then reserved for different subject matters is what marks the transition "from print to manuscript". As soon as manuscript production is no longer the default form of dissemination of knowledge, it takes on new meanings and establishes a different kind of literary community.

## Notes

1   For the digitisation project: http:/www.bilderhandschriften-digital. uni-hd.de follow the link to "Ludwig Henfflin". *Hans Wegener Beschreibendes Verzeichnis der deutschen Bilder-Handschriften des späten Mittelalters in der Heidelberger Universitätsbibliothek* (Leipzig, 1927), 71f., gives an overview of the common features of the manuscripts (scribes, illuminators and watermarks, available online: http://digi. ub.uni-heidelberg.de/diglit/Wegener1927/0079).

2   For a historical introduction to the literary background for Margaret of Savoy cf. Henrike Lähnemann, *Margarethe von Savoyen in ihren literarischen Beziehungen* in Encomia-Deutsch Berlin 2002, 158–173 (available online: http://www.icls.uni-freiburg.de/Publikationen/h._ lahnemann.pdf). The most extensive biographical data is in Gerhard Raff, Hie gut Wirtemberg allewege. Das Haus Württemberg von Graf Ulrich dem Stifter bis Herzog Ludwig, Stuttgart 1988.

3   Heidelberg UB, Cpg 17, f. 14$^r$. Text: I Sam 10 (http://digi.ub.uni-heidelberg.de/diglit/cpg17/0035).

4   Another possible candidate is Cpg 143 (Johann von Würzburg: 'Wilhelm von Österreich'), where planned illuminations were not executed and which is therefore excluded from his publication. Since, until the 19th century, one of the leaves from Cpg 345 (now f. 373a*) was erroneously bound into Cpg 143 as f. 267, the volumes were obviously kept side by side in an unbound stage. Brigitte Schöning, 'Friedrich von Schwaben'. *Aspekte des Erzählens im spätmittelalterlichen Versroman*, Erlangen 1991 (*Erlanger Studien 90*), therefore concluded that it had been part of Margaret's commission; Karin Zimmermann in her catalogue entry for the digital project (http://digi.ub.uni-heidelberg.de/sammlung2/werk/pdf/cpg143.pdf) argues against it, because the paper and the scribe are different from the Henfflin manuscripts. The parallel of the binding mistake which involved one manuscript from the Henfflin Workshop and one from the Lauber Workshop shows that the common storage in an unbound state does not presuppose the same origin. I have therefore excluded Cpg 143 from my survey although it might well have been part of Margaret's order.

5   For a detailed case study and figures about the surge of vernacular
    text printing cf. Romy Günthart, *Deutschsprachige Literatur im frühen
    Basler Buchdruck* (ca. 1470–1510) (*Studien und Texte zum Mittelalter
    und zur frühen Neuzeit,* vol. 11), 2007, especially 222 on manuscript
    copies from early Basel prints.

6   Heimo Reinitzer, 'Oberdeutsche Bibeldrucke (vollständige Bibeln)',
    in: *Die deutsche Literatur des Mittelalters, 2nd edition by Burghart
    Wachinger* (VL2), vol. 6 (1987), col. 1276–1289, here col. 1280.
    For a full discussion of a manuscript copy of a Mentelin Bible cf.
    Christine Wulf, *Eine volkssprachige Laienbibel des 15. Jahrhunderts.
    Untersuchung und Teiledition der Handschrift Nürnberg, StB, Ms. Solg.
    16.2°* (*Münchner Texte und Untersuchungen,* vol. 98), 1991; a short
    description of the Henfflin volumes on 25. All illuminated German
    Bible manuscripts are listed in the *Katalog der deutschsprachigen
    illuminierten Handschriften,* ed. by Norbert H. Ott, begun by Hella
    Frühmorgen-Voss. vol. 2, München 1996. The Henfflin Bible is Nr.
    14.0.5. An interesting feature is that there is one leaf from an earlier
    illuminated German Bible bound into the volumes, part of a set of
    manuscripts produced by Diebold Lauber (Katalog, Nr. 14.0.6.)
    which might have belonged to Margaret's second husband, Ludwig
    IV (Cpg 19–23). It represents a different branch of Bible translation
    (Walther XII); Mentelin belongs to Walther's branch 1. See also the
    manuscript description in: *Die erste deutsche Bibel,* ed. by William
    Kurrelmeyer, Tübingen 1915 (*Bibliothek des Litterarischen Vereins
    in Stuttgart,* vol. 266), vol. 10, xxix (he mentions seven manuscript
    copies of the Mentelin Bible while Reinitzer can name eight).

7   For the importance of the genealogical argument for the romance cf.
    the chapter "Friedrich von Schwaben – ein Herzog, wie er im Buche
    steht. Schwäbisches Landesbewusstsein und literarische Vermittlung"
    in Sandra Linden (ed., transl. and comm.), *Friedrich von Schwaben,
    Konstanz 2005* (Bibliotheca suevica, vol. 14), 469–492. Klaus Graf
    in his review (*Zeitschrift für deutsches Altertum,* vol. 129 (1999), 104–
    110) of Klaus Ridder, *Mittelhochdeutsche Minne- und Aventiureromane.
    Fiktion, Geschichte und literarische Tradition im späthöfischen Roman*:
    "Reinfried von Braunschweig", "Wilhelm von Österreich", "Friedrich
    von Schwaben", Berlin 1998 (*Quellen und Forschungen zur Literatur-
    und Kulturgeschichte,* vol. 12) wrote polemically against connecting the
    hero with the history of Württemberg but what might be true for the
    original text need not be true for the reception of it.

8   Additional devices: Cpg 76, f. 9v *fortuna,* abbreviated to F on f. 8$^r$, 10$^r$
    16$^v$, 17$^v$, 20$^r$ and 22$^r$, V (= Ulrich?) on f. 29$^r$, (M = Margaret?) on f.
    10$^r$, 11$^v$, 14$^r$, 21$^v$, 23$^v$ and 29$^r$. Cpg 345, f. 311$^r$: fortuna me mena alto
    fare lo mal e mi por (under the bottom line) and the coat of arms of
    Savoy (above the top line), f. 379$^r$: arms of alliance of Württemberg
    and Savoy.

9   The middle panel was probably destroyed during the Reformation, following the iconoclastic movement of the "Uracher Götzentag" (a meeting of the Lutheran ministers which requested the abolition of all idols and popish imagery) while the side-panels were kept. By 1593 these panels are still recorded as being in the castle, aptly in the bridal chamber, preserving the genealogical interest.

10  Thomas Fritz, *Ulrich der Vielgeliebte (1441–1480). Ein Württemberger im Herbst des Mittelalters. Zur Geschichte der württembergischen Politik im Spannungsfeld zwischen Hausmacht, Region und Reich* (Leinfelden, 1999) (*Schriften zur südwestdeutschen Landeskunde 25*). - "Mit allen 3. Gemahlinen lebte Gr. Ulrich vergnügt, sonderlich mit der letzteren." (Count Ulrich lived happily with all his three spouses, especially so with the last one) writes Pregizer at the beginning of the 18th century in his "Württemberg Cedar-Tree", Johann Ulrich Pregizer III, *Wirttembergischer Cedern-Baum, Oder Vollständige Genealogie Des Hoch-Fürstlichen Hauses Wirttemberg: In sechs Theilen / Aus denen besten und bewährtesten Autoribus und Genealogisten ... anfangs zusammen getragen und entworffen Von Weyland D. Johann Ulrich Pregitzern, Hoch-Fürstl. Wirtt. Ober- und Justiz-Rath ... Nachmahls elaboriret Und mit Historischen Anmerckungen vermehret ... Von dessen ältistem Sohn, gleichen Nahmens, ... Nach desselben Anno 1730. erfolgten Tod aber heraußgegeben und biß auf jetzige Zeiten fortgesetzt Von seinem jüngern Bruder, Johann Eberhard Pregitzern* (Stuttgart, 1734).

11  Sheila Edmunds, 'The medieval library of Savoy' *Scriptorium*, 24 (1970), 318–327; 25 (1971), 253–284; 26 (1972), 269–293. The widowed Amadeus was elected as an alternative Pope to Eugene IV by the Council of Basel in 1439 and although he exchanged the tiara for a Cardinal's hat in 1449 to make way for Nicholas V, Margaret thus became for ten years the only legitimate Pope's daughter of history.

12  Martin Le Franc: *Le champion des dames*, ed. by Robert Deschaux, Paris 1999 (Les classiques français du Moyen Age), vol. 5, 233, verse MMDXLIII–IV = ll. 20337–20360.

13  For example Guillaume de Deguileville: 'Pèlerinage de la vie humaine' (Cod. Pal. Lat. 1969, Parchment, 84 fol., 29,5x20,5cm, Toulouse 1375) from the collection of Louis I. of Anjou which might have come to the Palatine Library through Margaret. There is also a French manuscript of "Le champion des dames" in the Palatine Library (Heidelberg UB, Cpl 1968) of the work which has the praise for Margaret on f. 156v–157r. This might be a copy that Margaret brought with her to Heidelberg. However Martina Backes, *Das literarische Leben am kurpfälzischen Hof zu Heidelberg im 15. Jahrhundert. Ein Beitrag zur Gönnerforschung des Spätmittelalters* (Tübingen, 1992) (Hermaea N.F. 68), 181, pointed out that this copy lacks the praise for Amadé VIII and the verses on Margaret's mother, Marie de Bourgogne, and her sister, Bonne de Montfort, and only mentions her sister-in-law, Anne de Chypres (f. 15v).

14 Due to the bibliophile interests of the Palatine Electors Margaret's husband, Ludwig, among them there is a large number of Lauber manuscripts in Heidelberg, completely digitised on the same website (http://bilderhandschriften-digital.uni-hd.de, follow the link to "Diebold Lauber"); there has been a recent surge in interest in the Lauber manuscripts, following the publications of Lieselotte E. Saurma-Jeltsch, *Spätformen mittelalterlicher Buchherstellung. Bilderhandschriften aus der Werkstatt Diebold Laubers in Hagenau* (Wiesbaden, 2001), and Christoph Fasbender, 'húbsch gemolt – schlecht geschrieben? Kleine Apologie der Lauber-Handschriften' *Zeitschrift für deutsches Altertum und deutsche Literatur*, vol. 131 (2002), 66–78.

15 A good survey of the changes manuscript production was undergoing in the fifteenth century can be found in Norbert H. Ott, 'Die Handschriften-Tradition im 15. Jahrhundert' in *Die Buchkultur im 15. und 16. Jahrhundert*, ed. by Barbara Tiemann, vol. 1, Hamburg 1995 (*Veröffentlichung der Maximilian-Gesellschaft. Jahresgabe der Maximilian-Gesellschaft*), 47–124, especially the chapter on "Serielle Handschriftenproduktion in bürgerlichen Werkstätten", 73–86.

16 Biblia sacra. Deutsche Edition der Bibelausgabe des Hieronymus durch Johann Mentelin 1466 zu Strassburg gedruckt (1. gedruckte deutsche Bibel) nach einer Übersetzung um das Jahr 1350; mit reichhaltigen Summarien und Prologen sowie Anweisungen zur Erarbeitung des Grundtextes (Wiederabdruck nach der Inc. 2099 d. Staatsbibliothek Berlin, P*. - Berlin : Berndt, 1987).

17 The text of the second branch of German bible translation which was taken up by the Mentelin Bible is not published; the only easily accessible facsimile of a manuscript representing the branch is that of the so-called 'Wenzelsbibel' (Codices selecti LXX/1–9, Graz 1981–1991), cf. Heimo Reinitzer, 'Wenzelsbibel', in: VL2, vol. 10 (1999), col. 869–875. The Henfflin manuscript follows the text closely, but reduces the phrase Jdt 13,8 *zů einer seule die do was zů* ("to a column that was at") to a single *zů*, presumably by a slip of the eye (haplography), leaving the *ir* (= *die seule*) at the end of the verse without a reference.

18 This draft translation of the German version aims to keep the unevenness of the original which in itself is based on Jerome's deliberately rough translation prose for the Book of Judith (cf. Henrike Lähnemann, ›Hystoria Judith‹. *Deutsche Judithdichtungen vom 12. bis zum 16. Jahrhundert* (Berlin/New York, 2006) (*Scrinium Friburgense 20*), 74–80). The Vulgate version (following the Sixto-Clementina) for the passage: 13,8 Et cum hæc dixísset, accéssit ad colúmnam quæ erat ad caput léctuli ejus, et pugiónem ejus, qui in ea ligátus pendébat, exsólvit. 9 Cumque evaginásset illum, apprehéndit comam cápitis ejus, et ait : Confírma me, Dómine Deus, in hac hora. 10 Et percússit bis in cervícem ejus, et abscídit caput ejus, et ábstulit conópeum ejus a

colúmnis, et evólvit corpus ejus truncum. 11 Et post pusíllum exívit, et trádidit caput Holofērnis ancíllæ suæ, et jussit ut mítteret illud in peram suam. 12 Et exiérunt duæ, secúndum consuetúdinem suam, quasi ad oratiónem, et transiérunt castra, et gyrántes vallem....

19  On the *conopeum* in Judith cf. the article by Barbara Schmitz (in: *The Sword of Judith*. Cambridge: Open Book Publishing 2009).

20  There are only three branches that translate all of the Bible, including the Apocrypha, the first, second and twelfth which is the so-called "Wien-Zürcher Bibel" (cf. Heimo Reinitzer, in: VL2, vol.10 (1999), col. 1053–1057).

21  The rubricator erroneously labelled the figure of Judith as *Hester* in his caption for the image, thinking ahead to the Book of Esther that follows only a few pages later.

22  Henrike Lähnemann and Timo Kröner, 'Die Überlieferung des ›Sigenot‹. Bildkonzeptionen im Vergleich von Handschrift, Wandmalerei und Frühdrucken', *Jahrbuch der Oswald von Wolkenstein-Gesellschaft* 2003/2004, 175–188 (cf. the documentation on the web: http://www.staff.ncl.ac.uk/henrike.laehnemann/sigenot/).

23  John L. Flood, 'Studien zur Überlieferung des Jüngeren Sigenot‛, *Zeitschrift für deutsches Altertum*, 95 (1966), 42–79.

24  Henrike Lähnemann, 'Pontus und Sidonia', Heidelberger Universitätsbibliothek cpg 142. Literar- und kunsthistorische Einführung (München, 1999) (Codices illuminati medii aevi 49).

25  On the "developments in the informational content of the title-page" in the late 15th century cf. Margaret M. Smith, *The title-page, its early development, 1460–1510* (London, 2000), 108.

26  Peter Jörg Becker, *Handschriften und Frühdrucke mittelhochdeutscher Epen. Eneide, Tristrant, Tristan, Erec, Iwein, Parzival, Willehalm, Jüngerer Titurel, Nibelungenlied und ihre Reproduktion und Rezeption im späteren Mittelalter und in der frühen Neuzeit* (Wiesbaden, 1977).

27  Wegener (1927), 72.

28  Ute von Bloh, *'Historie von Herzog Herpin', übertragen aus dem Französischen von Elisabeth von Nassau Saarbrücken. Heidelberg, Universitäts-bibliothek Cod. Pal. Germ. 152* (München, 1990) (Codices illuminati medii aevi 17), 33–45.

*Opposite page and page 36*: Jost Amman 's illustrations from *Das Ständebuch* (1568), showing in sequence from top to bottom: the papermaker, the printer, the blockmaker and the bookbinder.

# GW 6002: A Typographical Conundrum from 1479

*John L. Flood*

This paper has a somewhat curious origin. It goes back perhaps some twenty years or so when my colleague, Bill Yuill (1921–1997), who was then a Professor of German in London, first at Bedford College and then at Royal Holloway College, gave me a small envelope which, he said, he had found stuck in the back of a cupboard when he was clearing out his office at the University of Nottingham, where he had held the Chair of German from 1966 to 1975. The envelope had the words 'Dietfurt. Print. GW 6002.', written in black ink on it, and inside was a small semi-transparent packet with the words, 'Das gute Spezialgeschäft FOTO BAER Dietfurt/ Opf.', printed on it with a rubber stamp. This contained twenty-four black-and-white photographs, each measuring 85 x 62 mms, though the actual image was only 75 x 52 mms. It was immediately evident to me that this set of photographs must have been left behind by Yuill's predecessor, Kenneth King, who had been Professor of German at Nottingham from 1952 to 1965. King was interested in early German printing. However the writing on the envelope was not in King's hand – I had been a pupil and colleague of his, so I knew it well. I am fairly confident now that it is the hand of Frederick Ratcliffe, the later Cambridge University Librarian, who had taken a PhD at Manchester under King's supervision (Ratcliffe 1952) and who wrote extensively on topics not unrelated to the matter in hand, though, as far as I can see, he never once mentioned this particular book.

I did not do anything about these photographs for many years, though I did look up the book in the *Gesamtkatalog der Wiegendrucke* (GW). It turns out to be the sole known copy, and indeed one of just a small number of incunabula in the Franciscan monastery at Dietfurt, according to ISTC. Its place of printing and the identity of the printer are unknown, though it is thought to have been printed at either Augsburg or Nuremberg on the grounds that, while the majority of the types are rather worn examples of the types used by Anton Koberger at Nuremberg, the upper-case F, Q and W correspond to those of Günther Zainer at Augsburg. According to GW, Zainer's types were used by other printers after his death in 1478. GW thus suggests that the book was printed by a small-scale printer who had acquired Koberger's and Zainer's old types.

Since the days of Ratcliffe and King the study of early German printing has made great strides, and I thought that this colloquium would provide a welcome opportunity to re-examine the problems associated with the book in question.

As already indicated, the book (GW 6002; ISTC ic00105300) appears to be unique. Its provenance, the Franciscan monastery at Dietfurt near Regensburg, does not tell us very much beyond suggesting that the book is more than likely to be of south German origin, which one might have guessed anyway. The monastery was not founded until 1660, so there is no point in attaching much significance to the book's current location.[1]

It contains the text of the Song of Songs in Latin and German. It is an interesting experiment in book design, as the colophon [Ill. 1] explains:

'This is Solomon's *Cantica canticorum*, called *Das Buch der Liebe* in German, that each man can read in Latin or in German as he pleases, the difference being that whoever wants to read the book in Latin, let him read the longer lines, but whoever wants to read it in German, let him read the shorter lines, and [it] is interpreted by the teachers of Holy Scripture as referring to our dear Virgin Mary, in praise of whom it has been translated into German and printed. Anno Domini one thousand four hundred and in the 79th year &c'

What the colophon attempts to explain is that whereas the Latin text occupies the full measure of the line, the German text is indented, so that it is easier to pick out. Such an arrangement (rather than printing the two versions in parallel columns or on facing pages) appears to be extremely rare.

There can be no doubt about the date: 'printed Anno Domini one thousand four hundred and in the 79th year.' This fits in intriguingly with what we know about the types. According to GW the text is basically printed in Anton Koberger's type 2, measuring 115 mm over twenty lines, used by him in Nuremberg until 1477. Again according to GW the upper-case letters F, Q and W correspond to Günther Zainer's type 2; he died at Augsburg in 1478.

When Koberger, who was to be the most important printer-publisher in Nuremberg until his death in 1513, actually started printing is not clear. He is known to have rented premises on the Egidienplatz to serve as a workshop and warehouse in 1470, but his first book, Albrecht von Eyb's *Ehebüchlein*, may not have appeared much before 16 October 1472.[2]

Günther Zainer was the first printer at Augsburg. There has been a valuable new study of his work by Akihiko Fujii (2007), but this has little bearing on our present enquiry because Zainer died in 1478, the year before the Song of Songs edition was produced. We can well imagine that, on Zainer's death, his equipment was disposed of, entire or piecemeal.

The evidence from the Song of Songs booklet suggests that we are really looking for a link between it and Augsburg or Nuremberg printers around 1478 and 1479. According to Geldner (1968–70: I, 146) Zainer's type 2 was used by the Augsburg printer, Ambrosius Keller, for an Aristotle (GW 2335) and for Gentilis Fulginas, *Quaestio de maiorite morbi* (GW 10623), both folios of 1479, and also by another Augsburg printer, Hermann Kaestlin, for a *Lucidarius* of 1481 (ISTC il00332260).[3] As for Koberger's type 2 this seems not to have been traced to any printer other than 'the printer of "Cantica canticorum"'; at least these types do not

Ill. 1: Fols 12r (last page of text) and 12v (colophon)

Ill. 2: Koberger's type 2, from BMC, III, p. XXXIX, is apparently dated 1478, though BMC, II, p. 409, says it was used from 1472 to 1477.

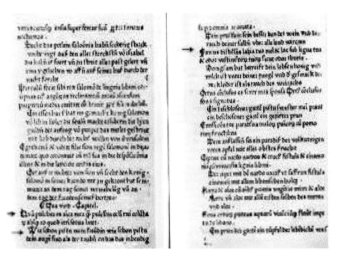

Ill. 3: Fols 4v and 6r, showing the Q, W and F of 'Zainer'.

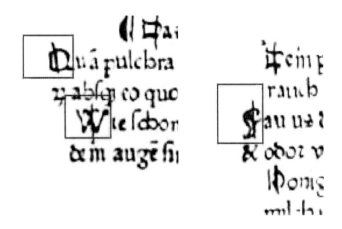

Ill. 4: The Q, W and F of 'Zainer' enlarged. It should be noted that initial upper-case letters have been picked out with a pen-stroke.

recur in the equipment of other small Nuremberg printers around 1480, such as Hans Folz.[4] It should be mentioned *en passant* that, though Dietfurt is close to Regensburg (about twenty-four miles away), the Song of Songs cannot have been printed there as printing was not introduced at Regensburg until 1485.

The booklet itself, a small quarto, gives little away. It has no title, let alone a title page, and there are no running headings, signatures, catchwords or pagination. The text is articulated only by the German headings marking the beginning of the chapters, 'Das ander Capitel', etc., but it should be noted that there is no heading before the first chapter, the heading for the second chapter is placed after verse fifteen of chapter one, instead of after verse sixteen, and that the heading marking the beginning of chapter three is lacking (though the headings for chapters four, five, six, seven and eight are correctly placed and numbered). The text is printed with twenty-six lines to a page. My photographs do not contain a scale, so it is not possible to ascertain the page size with accuracy, but since Koberger's type 2 measures 115 mm over twenty lines, the height of the printing area will have been approximately 145 mm. The width is c. 96 mm.

ISTC gives the printer simply as 'Printer of "Cantica canticorum"', which implies that no other book from this press has been identified. It seems unlikely that further analysis of the typography will throw much light on the origin of the book. However it is possible to approach it from two other angles. One is the book-historical context, and the other is the linguistic character of the text.

First the book-historical context. The Song of Songs, or Song of Solomon, is of course a biblical text, coming between Ecclesiastes and Isaiah in the Old Testament.[5] This bilingual edition appears to have been the only separate edition of the Song of Songs published in the incunable period; there are several sixteenth-century Latin editions printed in Germany in the British Library.[6] ISTC lists twenty-one incunabula relating to the Song of Songs, but with the sole exception of our bilingual edition these are all sermons or commentaries on the subject. Among them are six editions of the sermons of St Bernard of Clairvaux, three of Pope Gregory the Great's commentary, and five editions of the commentary of the Franciscan Nicholas of Lyra (c. 1270-1349) on the Psalter and the Song of Songs. Only two of these books were printed before 1479, the year in which GW 6002 appeared. These are Johannes Gerson, *De spiritualibus nuptiis, sive Commentum super Cantica canticorum*, Nuremberg: [Johann Sensenschmidt], 1470 (ISTC ig00272000) and one of the editions of Pope Gregory's commentary, [Cologne: Ulrich Zell, not after 1473] (ISTC ig00394000). Neither of these books would seem to have any direct relevance to the bilingual edition, though it may be worth noting that the Gerson was printed at Nuremberg, but nine years earlier.

Given the nature and date of our book, one obvious line of approach is to consider the bilingual Song of Songs against the background of Bible printing, for the time when the Song of Songs came out was a period when the printing of Bibles, whether in Latin or German, was already big business. Bible printing had begun in the early 1450s when Johann Gutenberg produced the two-volume Latin Bible now known as the Gutenberg Bible or the 42-line Bible (GW 4201). Completed by August 1456 at the latest, it was the first of ninety-four Latin Bibles printed in Europe in the fifteenth century. Of these no fewer than fifty seven appeared in German-speaking towns. Of the forty-five Latin Bibles that had been published by 1480 thirty-one had come from German presses: eight of them from Nuremberg, including six by Anton Koberger alone (GW 4218, 4227, 4232, 4234, 4239, 4243), making him the biggest Bible printer of the age.[7] Soon the Bible became so readily available that already in 1504 Koberger said of the edition printed for him by Johann Amerbach at Basle between 1498 and 1502, *Es ist warlich ein unkewfflich werck [...] der handel der bucher ist so gancz nichtz mer, das ich nicht weiß, was man machen möchte.*"[8]

Germany led the way in printing vernacular Bibles too, long before the Protestant Reformers, in asserting 'the priesthood of all believers', contended that all Christians had the right and duty to explore scriptural truth for themselves. The first vernacular Bible ever printed was the German Bible issued by the Strassburg publisher, Johann Mentelin, before 27 June 1466.[9] No fewer than seven German Bibles were available before the bilingual Song of Songs appeared in 1479, and ten High German editions were already on the market by 1485 when the Archbishop of Mainz attempted to ban the printing of German Bibles.[10] These were:

1. Strassburg: J. Mentelin, 1466
2. Strassburg: H. Eggestein [before 1470]
3. Augsburg: G. Zainer [c. 1475]
4. Augsburg: J. Pflanzmann [c. 1475]
5. Nuremberg: J, Sensenschmidt, 1476–8
6. Augsburg: G. Zainer, 1477
7. Augsburg: A. Sorg, 1477
8. Augsburg: A. Sorg, 1480
9. Nuremberg: A. Koberger, 1483
10. Strassburg: J. Grüninger, 1485

Strassburg, Augsburg and Nuremberg were all playing key roles, but, given the typographical features linking the Song of Songs to Augsburg and Nuremberg printers, it is these towns that are of particular interest here.

We do well to remember that making the Scriptures available in the vernacular was a contentious issue. In 1369, in the Edict of Lucca, Emperor Charles IV forbade Bible translation.[11] In 1408 in England Thomas Arundel, Archbishop of Canterbury, declared it heresy to undertake any new translation of the Scriptures or even to own any English version unless both the owner and the translation were formally approved by a bishop, and more than a century later William Tyndale, failing to win the support of Cuthbert Tunstall, Bishop of London, for an English Bible, fled to Germany, where he had his New Testament printed at Cologne and Worms. The growth of printing was seen by the authorities as a real threat: in 1470 the Paris theologian Guillaume Fichet, while acknowledging the benefits of printing, felt reminded of the Trojan Horse, and in 1479 Pope Sixtus IV authorised the Faculty of Theology at Cologne to keep a watch on the local printing presses. A few years later, on 22 March 1485, Berthold von Henneberg, Archbishop of Mainz, forbade the printing of vernacular Bibles on pain of excommunication, confiscation, and a fine of one hundred Gulden.[12] In his 'Gutenberg Song' of about 1480 the Nuremberg printer-poet-barber-surgeon Hans Folz (1435/40–1513), criticises clerics who translate the Scriptures *um ringez gellt* 'for a paltry sum' and specifically warns against the dissemination of the Bible in the vernacular:

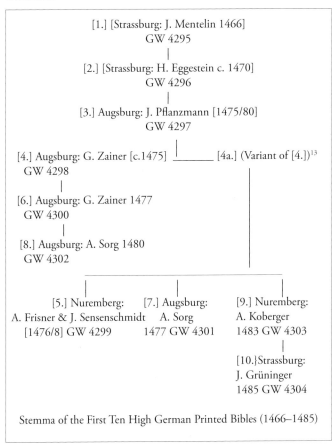

[1.] [Strassburg: J. Mentelin 1466]
GW 4295

[2.] [Strassburg: H. Eggestein c. 1470]
GW 4296

[3.] Augsburg: J. Pflanzmann [1475/80]
GW 4297

[4.] Augsburg: G. Zainer [c.1475] ——— [4a.] (Variant of [4.])[13]
GW 4298

[6.] Augsburg: G. Zainer 1477
GW 4300

[8.] Augsburg: A. Sorg 1480
GW 4302

[5.] Nuremberg:     [7.] Augsburg:     [9.] Nuremberg:
A. Frisner & J. Sensenschmidt    A. Sorg     A. Koberger
[1476/8] GW 4299        1477 GW 4301     1483 GW 4303

[10.}Strassburg:
J. Grüninger
1485 GW 4304

Stemma of the First Ten High German Printed Bibles (1466–1485)

'Many a layman is overfed with things he did not know about before and would never have dared ask about'.[14] At about the same time, perhaps at Nuremberg, a document was produced giving an opinion on the matter of vernacular translations. The unknown author states that, while it is recognised that printing can be of use to the Church, it can be the cause of poisonous errors, and the translation of theological works from Latin can be particularly dangerous. If Bible translations get into the hands of uneducated, inquisitive laymen, they might spurn hearing the word of God from the mouth of a priest and consider themselves cleverer than the priests. The translation of the Scriptures should be opposed, for the aim of such undertakings is to weaken the hierarchy of the church, to endanger orthodoxy, to sow confusion in Holy Church, lead souls into damnation, and destroy secular and ecclesiastical order.[15] It has been suggested that the document may represent a theological opinion sought by Anton Koberger as to the advisability of proceeding with a German Bible of his own; if it was, it did not dissuade him, for he brought out his edition, the ninth German Bible, on 17 February 1483 (GW 4303).

But while vernacular Scriptures were opposed by some or treated at least with circumspection by others, some people strongly supported their dissemination. For instance the third preface (of uncertain date but later fourteenth century) to the German adaptation of Nicholas of Lyra's commentary on the Psalter is a stout defence of making the Scriptures available to the wider public:

> Nu sind wenig leut latein gelert, davon ist, ob got wil uns hail geben, das man usz der latein zu deutsch pring, und halt in ander czungen, das die layen damit ze andacht pracht werden. Swer das irret und widerredet, der tut wider got, und vindet seinen lon darumb.[16]
>
> ('Few people are learned in Latin, so that if God wishes us well, it needs to be turned from Latin into German and be available in another tongue, so that the laity may be led to their devotions. Anyone who impedes that and speaks against it is acting against God and will reap his reward accordingly.')

Given the strong interest in Bibles and Bible translation in the Nuremberg area, we need to examine the German text of the Song of Songs to see how far it corresponds to the text of the early German Bibles. We cannot here examine the text in full, but I have selected at random one chapter, Chapter 6, for comparison, providing the Vulgate text, the text in Mentelin's German Bible of 1466 (with, as appropriate, significant variants from the later German Bibles of Pflanzmann, Zainer, and Koberger), and the text of the 1479 Song of Songs. Significant shared readings are indicated in **bold**, significant differences <u>underlined</u>.

**Chapter 6**       *1479: Das ist das sechst. Capitel*
*1 dilectus meus descendit in hortum suum ad areolam **aromatis** ut pascatur*

*in hortis et lilia colligat*
**1466**: *Mein lieber ist <u>abgestigen</u> in seinen garten zů dem betlein der* **aromathen**: *das er werd gefurt in den garten; vnd <u>lese</u> die liligen*
**1479**: *Mein lieb ist <u>nider gangen</u> in sein garten czu dē petlein der <u>edlen</u> <u>wurczen</u> das er ward im garten vnd das er <u>ab nem</u> dij lilgen*
2 *ego dilecto meo et dilectus meus mihi qui* **pascitur** *inter lilia*
**1466**: *Ich bin meim lieben: vnd mein lieber der ist mir: der do <u>wirt gefurt</u> vnter den liligen.*
Pflanzmann 1475/81: *gefůrt oder geweidtnot*; Zainer 1477: *wirt geweydet*
**1479**: *Jch meim liben vnd mein liber mir der* **geweidet** *wirt vnter den lilgen*
3 **pulchra es amica mea suavis et decora** *sicut Hierusalem terribilis ut* **castrorum acies** *ordinata*
**1466**: *Mein freundin du bist schön: senfft vnd geziert als jherusalem: vorcht sam als die <u>geordenten geselschafft der herbergen</u>.*
Pflanzmann 1475/81: *geselschafften*; Zainer 1477: *geordent ritterschar der gschloß*; Koberger 1483: *spitz der geschloß geordent*
**1479**: **Schon pistu mein freundin suß vnd wolgeschikte** <u>tochter</u> *von iherusalem forchsam als ein= | geordente* **spicz der schlosser** <u>kegen den feinden</u>
4 *averte oculos tuos a me quia ipsi me avolare fecerunt capilli tui sicut grex caprarum quae apparuerunt de Galaad*
**1466**: *Kere dein augen von mir: wann sy machen mich <u>hin zů fliegen</u>. Dein <u>locke</u> seint als die <u>herte der rechgaissen</u>: die do derscheinent von galaad.*
Pflanzmann 1475/81: *rechgeiß*
**1479**: *wend dein augen von mir sie haben mich <u>weck fliegen gemacht</u>. Dein <u>hor</u> als di <u>schar der geiß</u> di von galaad erschinen ist.*
5 *dentes tui sicut grex ovium quae ascenderunt de lavacro omnes gemellis fetibus et sterilis non est in eis*
**1466**: *Dein zen seint als die herte der schaff: die do <u>auffsteigen von der waschung</u>. All zwailinger geburt: vnd <u>vnperhaftigs</u> ist nit in in.*
**1479**: *Dein czen sein als die herd der schoff di <u>auß dē wasser gestigen</u> sein der czwilig vnd <u>vnfruchtbar</u> ist nit vnter in*
6 *sicut cortex mali punici genae tuae absque* **occultis tuis**
**1466**: *Dein <u>hůflein</u>[17] seint alz die rinde des rotten appfels <u>on deine augen</u>.*
Zainer 1477: *bäcklin.* Koberger 1483: *schelff*
**1479**: *Als di <u>schelff</u> deß czeitigen apfleß also sein dein <u>wangen</u> **an dein verborgē czir***
7 **sexaginta sunt reginae** *et octoginta concubinae et adulescentularum non est numerus*
**1466**: *Der kunigin waren lx: vnd der <u>kebsweib</u> lxxx: vnd der <u>iunglingin</u> was nit zal.*

Pflanzmann 1475/81: *iungling*, Zainer 1477: *iungen töchtern*
**1479**: **Sechsczig sind der kunigin** *vnd achtzig schlaffrauen vnd der iungen maidlein ist an czal.*

8 *una est columba mea perfecta mea una est matris suae electa genetrici suae viderunt illam filiae[18] et beatissimam praedicaverunt reginae et concubinae et laudaverunt eam*

**1466***: Die ein ist mein taube mein volkumen: sy ist ein ir mûter: ein derwelte ir gebererin. Die töchter von syon sahent sy vnd predigten sy die aller seligste: die kunigin vnd die kebsweiber die lobten sy.*

**1479***: Ain ist mein taub mein volkumene eine ist irer muter auserwelt irer gepererin. Die tochter von sion sahen sie vnd predigten di königin vnd die schlaffrauen lobten sie.*

9 *quae est ista quae progreditur quasi aurora consurgens pulchra ut luna electa ut sol terribilis ut castrorum acies ordinata*

**1466***: Wer ist die die do furget als der morgen rot aufsteigent: schön als die menin der welt als der sunn derschrockenlich als die geordenten geselschafft der herbergen?*

Zainer 1477: *die morgenröt; der mon; die sunne; geordenten ritterschafft der geschloß.*

Koberger 1483: *spitz der geschloß geordent*

**1479***: wer ist di die do aufget als di morgen rot di do aufsteigt schon als der mon auserwelt als die son forchtsam als ein geordente spicz der streiter*

10 *descendi ad **hortum nucum** ut viderem poma convallis ut inspicerem si floruisset vinea et germinassent mala punica*

**1466***: Ich staig ab in meinen garten daz ich sech die öpffel der teler: das ich schaute ob der weingart het geblûet: vnd die rotten öpffel hetten gekeimt.*

Zainer 1477: *gegronet*

**1479***: Jch ging nider in den **nußgarten** das ich sehe das obß des tals vnd das ich ansehe ob di wein garten hetten geplut vnd außhetten gebrochē die volkurnigen roten apfelpavm*

11 *nescivi anima mea conturbavit me propter quadrigas Aminadab*

**1466***: Ich west sein nit. Mein sel betrûbt mich: vmb die wegen aminadabs*

**1479***: Jch west sein nicht mein sele betrubet mich vnd die wagen aminadab*

12 *revertere revertere **Sulamitis** revertere revertere ut intueamur te*

**1466***: kere wider ker wider **sunamit***: kere wider ker wider das wir dich schauen.*

Zainer 1477: *anschauwen*

**1479***: Ker wider ker wid' suse tochter ker wider das wir dich anschawen*

It is evident from even this short passage that the 1479 Song of Songs version cannot descend from the 1466 Strassburg Bible or any of its derivatives. It is a separate translation. Often the Song of Songs follows the word order of the Latin more closely than do the German Bibles, e.g.

> 6,3 *pulchra es amica mea* and **1479**: *Schon pistu mein freundin* but **1466**: *Mein freundin du bist schön*
>
> 6,6 *sicut cortex mali punici genae tuae* and **1479**: *Als die schelff deß czeitigen apfleß also sein dein wangen* but **1466**: *Dein húflein seint alz die rinde des rotten appfels*
>
> 6,7 *sexaginta sunt reginae et octoginta concubinae* and **1479** *Sechsczig sind der kunigin vnd achtzig schlaffrauen* but **1466**: *Der kunigin waren lx: vnd der kebsweib lxxx.*

In other respects too the Song of Songs is sometimes closer to the Vulgate than the German Bibles are, e.g. in 6,2, where *pascitur* is translated by *geweidet* and in 6,10 where *hortum nucum* is precisely rendered by *nußgarten*. In fact the Song of Songs is based on a redaction of the Vulgate that was slightly different from that used by the German Bibles, for in 6,6 it renders *absque occultis tuis* by *an dein vorborgē czir* while the German Bibles have *on deine augen*, which points back to that group of Vulgate witnesses that read *absque oculis tuis* instead of *absque occultis tuis*.[19] The independence of the Song of Songs translation is clear from 6,3, where *ut castrorum acies ordinata* is rendered very differently by the Song of Songs and the German Bibles:

> **1466**: *als die geordenten geselschafft der herbergen*
>
> **1479**: *als ein geordente spicz der schlosser kegen den feinden*

and similarly at 6,9, where *ut castrorum acies ordinata* is rendered in the Song of Songs as *als ein geordente spicz der streiter* while the 1466 Bible has *als die geordenten geselschafft der herbergen*. The Authorized Version in English renders the Latin with 'as an army with banners'. It is clearly a difficult phrase and the Song of Songs translator and the German Bible translator have chosen different approaches. Interestingly Koberger in 1483 alters the text and makes it read very similarly to the Song of Songs when, at both points in the text, he has *spitz der geschloß*. We may note also that in 6,6 both the Song of Songs and Koberger translate *cortex* 'apple peel' by *schelff*, whereas the earlier German Bibles have *rinde*. This raises the question, which we cannot go into here, whether, when Koberger was going over Zainer's 1477 Bible, revising the text for his edition of 1483, the Song of Songs version may have been consulted. At least it tends to link the Song of Songs text with the Nuremberg area.

So the Song of Songs text is not textually related to the printed German Bibles, but where did it come from? At one point I thought that it might be related to a Song of Songs translation that is widely attested in manuscript. The oldest of these manuscripts, containing a bilingual text, with a segment of the Latin text followed by a German version, appears to be the 14th-century Cod. Osek 18 in Prague, Státni knihovna, fols 126ʳ–159ᵛ. Beyond this there are about eighteen further manuscripts, nearly all from the fifteenth century, mostly preserved in Austria, and all in Bavarian-Austrian dialect.[20] Attention was first drawn to this version by

Bartelmez in her 1972 study of Williram (d. 1085), Abbot of Ebersberg's, paraphrase of the Song of Songs.[21] A characteristic of these manuscripts is that the passage 6,4b–6,7 was lacking, possibly because these lines are largely a repetition of 4,1b–5.[22] The passage in question appears to be intact in the 1479 printed text, so it seems unlikely that it is closely related to any of these manuscript versions. Nevertheless we should note a couple of interesting textual correspondences. The first of these is 8,5b, a passage that gets 'amended' because it seems indelicate:

> **Vulgate**: *sub arbore malo suscitavi te <u>ibi corrupta</u> est mater tua <u>ibi violata</u> est genetrix tua* (which the Authorized Version in English delicately renders as: 'I raised thee up under the apple tree: there thy mother brought thee forth: there she brought thee forth that bare thee')
>
> **Graz 1132** (and others): *sub arbore malo suscitavi te <u>incorrupta</u> est mater tua <u>inviolata</u> est genetrix tua*

In the German text in Ms. Graz 1132 *incorrupta* is rendered by *unverderbet*, but it then has *genatczoget* which corresponds to the Vulgate's *violata*, not its own Latin *inviolata*. The corresponding passages in the **1479** Song of Songs read:

> *sub arbore malo sustentavi te ibi **corrupta** est mater tua <u>inviolata</u> est genetrix tua*
>
> *Vnter einē apfelpaū hab ich deī gewart do ist **gemailigt** dein muter do ist <u>beraupt</u> deī gepererī*

What is noteworthy here is that *beraupt* translates *violata*, not *inviolata*! Also of interest is 4,1b (cf. also 6,4):

> **Vulgate**: *capilli tui sicut greges caprarum* ['Thy hair is like herds of goats']
>
> **1479**: *Capilli tui sicut grex caprarum* ['Thy hair is like a herd of goats']
>
> *Daz har ist <u>hert als ein scar der geiß</u>* ['The hair is hard like a herd of goats']

The German here needs to be compared with the renderings in some of the manuscripts:

> **Graz 1132**: *dein har ist als ein hert ctzigen*
>
> **Graz 969** (from Seckau in Styria): *dein har ist hert als der geys*
>
> **Munich BSB Cgm 5377** (of unknown provenance) and **Munich BSB Clm 12723** (from Ranshofen, near Braunau am Inn): *dein har <u>ist hert als ein schar der gaiß</u>*

As Schmid (1992: 204) observes, the cause of these erroneous readings is the homophony of the noun *hert* 'herd' and the adjective *hert* 'hard'. The close similarity of 1479 and the two Munich manuscripts is striking.[23]

Yet, notwithstanding these correspondences, investigation of the remaining readings cited by Schmid (1992: 202–205) shows that the similarities are only sporadic and certainly do not add up to a convincing case for seeing the printed text as being especially closely related to any of these manuscript versions. The 1479 text was not a fresh, independent translation, however, but, as I hope to show, a witness to a much older version. For there is one manuscript to which it does seem to be related: Wiesbaden, Hessische Landesbibliothek, Cod. 52, fols. 381$^v$–388$^r$, a Ripuarian manuscript, written in 1469.[24] Let us look at Chapter 6 again, comparing 1479 and Wiesbaden Cod. 52 with the 1466 Bible once more. Once again significant shared readings are indicated in **bold**, significant differences underlined.

## Chapter 6

*1 dilectus meus descendit in hortum suum ad areolam **aromatis** ut pascatur in hortis et lilia colligat*

**1466**: *Mein lieber ist abgestigen in seinen garten zů dem betlein der **aromathen**: das er werd gefurt in den garten; vnd lese die liligen*

**1479**: *Mein lieb ist **nider gangen** in sein garten czu dē petlein der **edlen** wurczen das er ward im garten vnd das er ab nem dij lilgen*

**Wiesb. 52**: *[M]yn lyeff ys **nyder gegangen** yn synen bongarten zo den betten syner **edeler** cruder dat he **weyde** yn sy [?] dem bomgart vnd lylien lese*

*2 ego dilecto meo et dilectus meus mihi qui **pascitur** inter lilia*

**1466**: *Ich bin meim lieben: vnd mein lieber der ist mir: der do wirt gefurt vnter den liligen.*

**1479**: *Jch meim liben vnd mein liber mir der **geweidet** wirt vnter den lilgen*

**Wiesb. 52**: *Ich mynē lieff vnd myn lieff myr der da **weydet** vnder den lilien*

*3 pulchra es amica mea suavis et decora sicut Hierusalem terribilis ut **castrorum acies** ordinata*

**1466**: *Mein freundin du bist schön: senfft vnd geziert als jherusalem: vorcht sam als die **geordenten** geselschafft der herbergen.*

**1479**: *Schon pistu mein freundin suß vnd wolgeschikte tochter von iherusalem forchsam als ein= | **geordente spicz der schlosser** kegen den feinden*

**Wiesb. 52**: *Schone bistu vrundynnen myne soisse vnd wail gezyert als iherusalem untsienlich[25] als **deyn geordyneirde** schare der stryder[26]*

*4 averte oculos tuos a me quia ipsi me avolare fecerunt capilli tui sicut grex caprarum quae apparuerunt de Galaad*

**1466**: *Kere dein augen von mir: wann sy machen mich hin zů fliegen. Dein locke seint als die herte der rechgaissen: die do derscheinent von galaad.*

**1479**: *wend dein augen von mir sie haben mich **weck fliegen gemacht**. Dein hor als di schar der geiß di von galaad erschinen ist.*

**Wiesb. 52**: *kere abe dyne augen van myr want sy haynt mich wech vliegende gemacht Dyn **hayr** ist als herden der geyssen die in vffenbairdē von galaad*

*5 dentes tui sicut grex ovium quae ascenderunt de lavacro omnes gemellis fetibus et sterilis non est in eis*

**1466**: *Dein zen seint als die herte der schaff: die do <u>auffsteigen von der waschung</u>. All zwailinger geburt: vnd <u>vnperhaftigs</u> ist nit in in.*

**1479**: *Dein czen sein als die herd der schoff di <u>auß dē wasser gestigen</u> sein der czwilig vnd <u>vnfruchtbar</u> ist nit vnter in*

**Wiesb. 52**: *Dyne zende synt als eyn herde schaeffe die da <u>gegangen synt van der weschongen</u> Sy hayn alle zwillinge vnd da is <u>ekeyn gelde</u> vnder yn*

*6 sicut cortex mali punici genae tuae **absque occultis tuis***

**1466**: *Dein <u>húflein</u> seint alz die <u>rinde</u> des rotten appfels <u>on deine augen</u>.*

**1479**: *Als die **<u>schelff</u>** deß czeitigen apfleß also sein dein **wangen an dein verborgē czir***

**Wiesb. 52**: *Dyn **wangen** synt gelych deir <u>schurtzen</u> eyner prumegranaten sonder dat da ynwendich **verborgen** ist*

*7 sexaginta sunt reginae et octoginta concubinae et adulescentularum non est numerus*

**1466**: *Der kunigin waren lx: vnd der <u>kebsweib</u> lxxx: vnd der <u>iunglingin</u> was nit zal.*

**1479**: *Sechsczig sind der kunigin vnd achtzig <u>schlaffrauen</u> vnd der **iungen maidlein** ist an czal.*

**Wiesb. 52**: *Seszich synt der konyngynnen vnd achtzich der <u>amyē</u> der **ionger megdegen** en is keyner[27] zale*

*8 una est columba mea perfecta mea una est matris suae electa genetrici suae viderunt illam filiae et beatissimam praedicaverunt reginae et concubinae et laudaverunt eam*

**1466**: *Die ein ist mein taube mein volkumen: sy ist ein ir mûter: ein derwelte ir gebererin. Die töchter von syon sahent sy vnd predigten sy die aller seligste: die kunigin vnd die <u>kebsweiber</u> die lobten sy.*

**1479**: *Ain ist mein taub mein volkumene eine ist irer muter auserwelt irer gepererin. Die tochter von sion sahen sie vnd predigten di königin vnd die <u>schlaffrauen</u> lobten sie.*

**Wiesb. 52**: *eyne is myne duue myne volkomen eyne is yrer moder vsserkoren yrer gebererynnen Dye doichter van syon haynt sy[28] gesyen vnd sagent sy aller selichste Dye konynginnē vnd die <u>amyē</u> loueden sy*

*9 quae est ista quae progreditur quasi aurora consurgens pulchra ut luna electa ut sol terribilis ut castrorum **acies ordinata***

**1466**: *Wer ist die die do furget als <u>der</u> morgen rot aufsteigent: schön als di<u>e menin</u> der welt als <u>der</u> sunn <u>derschrockenlich</u> als <u>die geordenten geselschaffi der</u> -ol- > <u>herbergen</u>?*

**1479**: *wer ist di die do aufget als <u>di</u> morgen rot di do aufsteigt schon als der mon auserwelt als die son forchtsam als **ein geordente <u>spicz</u> der streiter***

**Wiesb. 52**: *Wer is der dar zo komet als die dagerait die da vff clymet schone als de maene vsserkoren als dye sonne vntsyenlich **als eyne geordinyerde***

*schar* **der stryder**

*10 descendi ad* **hortum nucum** *ut viderem poma convallis ut inspicerem si floruisset vinea et germinassent mala punica*

> **1466**: *Ich* <u>staig ab</u> *in meinen* <u>garten</u> *daz ich sech die* <u>öpffel</u> *der teler: das ich schaute ob der weingart het geblúet: vnd die rotten öpffel hetten* <u>gekeimt</u>.

> **1479**: *Jch* **ging nider** *in den* **nußgarten** *das ich sehe das* **obß** *des tals vnd das ich ansehe ob di wein garten hetten geplut vnd* <u>außhetten gebrochē</u> *die volkurnigen roten apfelpavm*

> **Wiesb. 52**: *Jch trat* **nyddert** *in den* <u>bongart</u> *dat ich dat* **oifß** *der dalen gesege / vnd abe dye wyn gart gebloeet hetten vnd abe die baume der prumegernaten spruyssen*

*11 nescivi anima mea conturbavit me propter quadrigas Aminadab*

> **1466**: *Ich west sein nit. Mein sel betrúbt mich: vmb die wegen aminadabs*

> **1479**: *Jch west sein nicht mein sele betrubet mich vnd die wagen aminadab*

> **Wiesb. 52**: *Jch en wystes nyet myne sele bedroyffde mich durch die wagē rydunge amynadaps*

*12 revertere revertere* **Sulamitis** *revertere revertere ut intueamur te*

> **1466**: *kere wider ker wider* **sunamit**: *kere wider ker wider das wir dich* **schauen**.

> **1479**: *Ker wider ker wid' <u>suse tochter</u> ker wider das wir dich* **anschawen**

> **Wiesb. 52**: *kere wyder kere wyder dat wyr dych* <u>beschudden</u>

The readings that stand out are:

6,1: *abgestigen* **1466** ~ *nider gangen* **1479**, *nyder gegangen* **Wiesb. 52**
*aromathen* **1466** ~ *edlen wurczen* **1479**, *edeler cruder* **Wiesb. 52**

6,4: *sy machen mich hin zŭ fliegen* **1466** ~ *sie haben mich weck fliegen gemacht* **1479**, *sy haynt mich wech vliegende gemacht* **Wiesb. 52**

6,9: *als die geordenten geselschafft der herbergen* **1466** ~ *als ein geordente spicz der streiter* **1479**, *als eyne geordinyerde schar der stryder* **Wiesb. 52**

Although this Ripuarian manuscript is far removed in dialect from our printed Song of Songs edition, there certainly seems to be a textual relationship, however obscure, between them.

GW 6002 is clearly in Upper German, not Ripuarian. The colophon alone (see Ill. 1 above), the only passage of which we may confidently say that it must reflect the printer's (as opposed to the translator's) spelling, shows the following features:

| | |
|---|---|
| b > p | puch |
| iu > eu | deutsch |
| uo > u | puch |
| ie --> | lieb, liben |
| î > ei | latein |

| z- > cz- | czu, czeilen, kurczen |
| -ul- | sulcher |
| ei > ai, ei | vnterschaid, heiligen |
| û > au | taussent |

These features, and others, for example *w* > *b*, a characteristic feature of Bavarian, e.g. 1,10 *geburmelt (= gewurmelt)*;[29] 5,3 *gebaschen (= gewaschen)*, occur consistently throughout the text, in fact, which may suggest that the language of the translation itself has been regularised by the printer, too. Nevertheless it seems that we are looking for an Upper German, more specifically a Bavarian/Austrian translator. But are we any nearer identifying him? I was struck by the chance reading of a statement made in 1993 by Kurt Gärtner: 'Der österreichische Bibelübersetzer eröffnet in der religiös bewegten Zeit Ludwigs des Bayern, vermutlich unterstützt von den Franziskanern eine neue Epoche der deutschen Bibelübersetzung'.[30] Could the fact that the only known copy of the Song of Songs translation survives in a Franciscan monastery (even though it was founded only in 1660) be a further pointer to the Franciscan link? And does the fact that the language of the Song of Songs is Bavarian/Austrian perhaps point also to 'der österreichische Bibelübersetzer', the 'Austrian Bible Translator'?[31] Indeed I am struck not only by the similarity of the spellings in the Song of Songs to those in works attributed to this man, the Song of Songs itself seems to fit very neatly into what we know of the scope of his work.

The 'Austrian Bible translator', also known as the 'der österreichische Anonymus', 'the Anonymous Austrian', was a mid-fourteenth-century (post-1330) writer, the extent of whose work is only now being gradually unearthed.[32] He appears to have been an educated layman, perhaps to be localised in the Danube area between Passau and Krems, who may have enjoyed the support of the Franciscans.[33] Thanks to recent discoveries by Kurt Gärtner, Gisela Kornrumpf and Freimut Löser in particular, his writings, surviving in mostly fifteenth-century manuscripts, are now seen to include:[34]

- a number of eschatological and heresiological tracts, known only from Vienna ÖNB Cod. 2846, written in 1478 and owned by one Ortolf von Trenbach (1440–1502);
- a harmonised translation of the gospels, Acts of the Apostles 1–5, and the apocryphal Gospel of Nicodemus, and written not later than 1330[35];
- a translation (of somewhat later date) of parts of the Old Testament, including Genesis, Exodus, Tobias, Daniel, and Job;
- a 'Sermo de corpore Cristi';
- parts of Revelation;
- excerpts from the apocryphal books Wisdom and Ecclesiasticus, preserved in Vienna ÖNB Cod. 2846 again;
- and – and this is possibly the most interesting in our present context – scattered quotations from Proverbs and Ecclesiastes.

Klapper (1938: 101) already suggested that these quotations might stem from a fuller commentary or translation.

And, if Löser is correct, to this list we must now also add the German version of the Psalm commentary, written by the Franciscan Nicholas of Lyra.[36] Gärtner praises the 'Anonymous Austrian' as one of the most able translators between Williram in the eleventh century and Luther in the sixteenth.[37]

Ill. 6: Area where the 'Anonymous Austrian Bible translator' worked?

Given that the 'Austrian Anonymous' appears to have translated extensive parts of the Old Testament and of the Old Testament apocrypha, including Job, Proverbs and Ecclesiastes, which immediately precede the Song of Solomon, and Daniel which comes later, it seems to me very possible that the Song of Songs translation may be a further relic of this man's activity. Another text ascribed to the 'Anonymous Austrian', but not mentioned by Löser, is a translation of Isaiah 12, which is preserved in Vienna Cod. 2847, fol. 307ʳ.[38] Isaiah is the book immediately following the Song of Songs in the Old Testament. To my mind all this underlines the validity of Löser's surmise that the corpus of biblical translations ascribable to him must surely have been more extensive than we can see at present: 'Es deutet sich – nach den sukzessiven Funden der jüngsten Zeit – ein Komplex biblischer Bücher an, der mit Sicherheit noch umfangreicher war, als wir heute sehen können' (Löser (2003: 696)). It seems to me at least very possible that the German text of the Song of Songs, GW 6002, is another stray piece of the Anonymous Austrian Bible translator's work, extracted from some manuscript and printed most probably by some small, equally anonymous printer in Nuremberg or nearby. As such, though it is not textually related to the printed German Bibles of the time, it nevertheless does fit into the general climate of a desire for reading the Scriptures in the vernacular.

When considering the question of the purpose of the group of bilingual Song of Songs manuscripts from the fourteenth and fifteenth centuries and their readership, Hans-Ulrich Schmid felt that the bilingual format made the text unsuitable for continuous reading, whether for private devotional reading or for use in a monastic community. While its bilingual character might suggest its use in a school context, Schmid considers this unlikely, seeing that the language of the Song of Songs is not easy and the erotic nature of its subject matter was problematic – after all, medieval exegetes had long specifically warned against a literal understanding of this particular text. This seems to be reflected even in the rather anxious statement in the colophon of the printed edition that the text 'is interpreted by the teachers of Holy Scripture as referring to our dear Virgin Mary, in praise of whom it has been translated into German and printed'. Schmid (1992: 205–6) thinks the Song of Songs text was intended for the instruction of adult monks for whom the Latin and German versions provided the basis for exegetical explication. That may have been the case with the manuscript versions, but whether it also accounts for the printed edition of 1479 we cannot tell.

As a printed book GW 6002 remains stubbornly singular and unique, which may perhaps reflect the precarious nature of printing this kind of material at this time. However, for all that further investigations are required, I hope to have shown that at least in textual terms it fits into a much broader picture. The many questions surrounding it will probably never be answered. The conundrum remains.

**Notes**

1   The monastery is currently a 'Zen meditation centre' (see www.dietfurt.de).
2   For details see Reske (2007: 655–7).
3   Geldner (1968: I, 146) refers to VGT, plates 466 and 592 for Keller and 467, 593 and 594 for Kaestlin, but these are perhaps not entirely convincing.
4   For the types used by Folz, who began printing in 1479, see VGT, plates 652–654. In the absence of any secondary literature on this Song of Songs edition, we may presume that in assigning the books to Augsburg or Nuremberg GW was guided solely by typographical criteria. At least, there is no evidence that anyone has examined the language of the German text, specifically its graphemics. Fujii (2007) has painstakingly analysed the development of spelling in Günther Zainer's workshop in Augsburg, on the basis of eighteen books printed between 1471 and c.1478, noting chronological developments in the graphemic system and in particular having regard to any variation within a book which may indicate a change of compositor. Among the books are the German Bibles of 1475/6 (ISTC ib00627000) and 1477 (ISTC ib00629000), on which see below.
5   For the Song of Songs in the Middle Ages see Ohly (1958); also Kurt

Ruh, in VL², IV, cols 84–91; XI, col. 690.

6    See German STC (1962: 103–4).

7    Of the other Latin Bibles from German presses seven were produced in Cologne, six in Basle, five in Strassburg, three in Mainz and one each in Bamberg and Ulm.

8    See Widmann (1965: II, 141).

9    The Mentelin Bible is perhaps related to the 'Wenzelsbibel', an incomplete translation of the Old Testament made for Wenzel, King of Bohemia, (d. 1419), of which Vienna ÖNB Cod. 2759–2764 appears to be an incomplete copy. See VL², X, cols. 869–75; also Ratcliffe (1989: 33).

10   In 1478/79 two further Bibles, in regional dialects, appeared at Cologne. These are not relevant to the present enquiry.

11   Mentioned by Ratcliffe (1965a: 64), where reference is made to Burdach (1924: 30).

12   For early reactions to the printing of Bibles in German see Flood (2005: 25).

13   For details of the variant setting see GW, IV, col. 165. Also Kurrelmeyer (1900); Flood (1999).

14   Flood (2005: 24); for the text of the 'Gutenberg-Lied' ibid. 13–19.

15   *Avisamentum salubre quantum ad exercicium impressorie literarum*, Munich BSB: clm. 901, fols. 202ʳ–205ᵛ. For further details and discussion see Flood (2005: 25–27).

16   Ratcliffe (1965a: 56–7), lines 48-52. Ratcliffe, who believed that the German commentary was the work of Heinrich von Mügeln, argued that this third preface may not be original and thus not necessarily by Mügeln himself (71–74). Ratcliffe (1961: 430ff.) identified some forty textual witnesses to the German Psalm commentary, among them two printed editions from 1475 (Hain *13508) and 1504 (VD16 B 3268).

17   Williram of Ebersberg uses the word *huffelon*; Prague, Státni knihovna, Cod. Osek 18, a fourteenth-century Song of Songs text, also uses *hüffel* as well as *wangen*. See Schmid (1992: 207).

18   There is no mention of Sion in the Vulgate at this point.

19   According to the critical apparatus in *Biblia Sacra iuxta Vulgatam Versionem*, 1969, II, 1000, redactions CAZbk read *oculis* instead of *occultis*.

20   Thirteen of these are noted by Schmid (1992: 199–208). Additional ones are noted by Reinitzer and Kornrumpf, 'Salomonische Schriften', VL², XI, cols. 1358–1368, here col. 1365.

21   Bartelmez (1972). Schmid (1992: 199–201) agreed that the Latin text in the manuscripts ultimately goes back to the Latin text used by Williram but showed that the German text could not be regarded as a descendant from Williram's translation.

22   Schmid (1992), reviewing Bartelmez's findings, ascertained that

this passage was omitted in all the manuscript witnesses but one, a late 14th-century Ms. 1132 in Graz, originally from the Cistercian monastery at Neuberg. According to Schmid, the scribe of Graz Ms. 1132 noticed the omission and supplied the missing passage from another source, actually adding more text than had originally been omitted.

23 One further, though somewhat tenuous, link with Clm 12723 is in 4,16 where 1479 and Clm 12723 call the north wind *aquilo*, using the Latin name found in the Vulgate, but 1479 similarly calls the south wind *auster* while Clm 12723 leaves a blank; the other Munich manuscript, Cgm 5377, leaves a blank for both. For further details of this interesting textual crux see Schmid (1992: 204).

24 See Heimo Reinitzer and Gisela Kornrumpf, 'Salomonische Schriften', in VL², XI, cols. 1358–68, here col. 1365. This translation was noted by Kurt Ruh, in VL², IV, col. 88. Ruh seems to have been unaware of GW 6002. For a description of Wiesbaden Cod. 52 see Zedler (1931: 63–64). The Song of Songs is followed on fols 388ʳ–389ʳ by the beginning of a German version of a Dutch commentary on it. The manuscript was completed 'on St Paulinus's day' (presumably 31 August, the Feast of St Paulinus, Bishop of Trier, d. 358) 1469; it came from the Cistercian convent at Schönau (near Gemünden in Bavaria) but, on linguistic grounds, it cannot have been written there.

25 *untsienlich* is an uncertain reading.

26 *deyn* is written, but the *d* appears to be crossed through to correct the reading to *eyn*.

27 Or perhaps *keyne*, the *r* possibly being struck through.

28 The first instance of *sy* is inserted above the base line as a correction.

29 *geburmelt* (=*gewurmelt*), meaning 'vermiculated, with wormholes; inlaid with small stones'.

30 Cited by Löser (2003: 689). My emphasis. Ludwig IV, 'der Bayer', was Holy Roman Emperor from 1328 to 1347.

31 Cf. his critical comment on philosophers: *was nement sich dann dy armen philossopheir an, die vnzeittleich wider den cristentumb redent vnd wänent, sy mugen jr red mit maisterschaft, die valsch ist, wider guet gemachen. czbar: sy sein prennenswert als ander keczer.* Cited by Löser (2003:706). Other -cz- spellings of the 'Anonymous Austrian' occur in Vienna ÖNB Cod. 2846, e.g. *verczerent*, cited by Löser (2003: 699). On this manuscript see Bergeler (1944). On the 'Austrian Bible Translator' see also Knapp (1999: 215–233) and the following, more specialised studies: Kornrumpf (1991); Löser (1991), Kornrumpf, 'Österreichischer Bibelübersetzer', VL², XI, cols 1097–1110; Kornrumpf (2004); and Beck (2007).

32 On the date see Freimut Löser, 'Schlierbacher Altes Testament', VL², VIII, cols. 720–726, here col. 721.

33 See Kornrumpf, VL², XI, col. 1098.

34 For fuller details see Löser (2003: 693–697).

35 Löser (2003: 695).

36 See Löser (2003: 697-708). Heinrich von Mügeln's authorship of the Psalm commentary, while asserted in the oldest dated manuscript, is no longer generally accepted. The validity of the attribution was doubted by Kurt Gärtner, 'Zur Herkunft der Psalmenübersetzung im 'Psalmenkommentar' Heinrichs von Mügeln', in: Plate / Rapp (2004), 97–106.

37 Kurt Gärtner, in VL², IV, cols 1253–4.

38 The text begins: *Hie hebent sich an die Cantica der propheten, von erst Ysaias. Confitebor tibi, domine, quoniam iratus es michi, conuersus est furor. Herr ich vergich dir, wan du pist erczürnt gen mir.* (Again one notes the characteristic spellings *-cz-* and *p-*.) The principal content of Cod. 2847, which was written c. 1420/30, is the 'Anonymous Austrian's' German version of the Psalm commentary of Nicholas of Lyra. It also contains German versions of the Magnificat and the Nunc dimittis. See Menhardt (1960: I, 420)

## Bibliography

Bartelmez, Erminnie Hollis (1972): 'Williram's Text of the Song of Solomon and its distribution', *Manuscripta*, 16, 165–168.

Beck, Wolfgang (2007): 'Neue Fragmente des 'Psalmenkommentars' des Österreichischen Bibelübersetzers aus dem Staatsarchiv Altenburg/ Thüringen', *Zeitschrift für deutsches Altertum und deutsche Literatur*, 136,1: 68–71.

Bergeler, Alfred (1944): 'Kleine Schriften Heinrichs von Mügeln im Cod. Vind. 2846', *Zeitschrift für deutsches Altertum*, 80: 177–184.

BMC = *Catalogue of Books Printed in the XVth Century Now in the British Museum*, London: British Museum, 1908–2007.

Burdach, Konrad (1924): *Die nationale Aneignung der Bibel und die Anfänge der Germanischen Philologie*, Halle: Niemeyer.

Flood, John L. (1999): 'Les premières Bibles allemandes dans le contexte de la typographie européenne des XVe et XVIe siècles' in: *La Bible imprimée dans l'Europe moderne*, ed. Bertrand Eugene Schwarzbach, (Etudes et recherches), Paris: Bibliothèque nationale de France, 144–65.

Flood, John L. (2005): 'Hans Folz zwischen Handschriftenkultur und Buchdruckerkunst' in: *Texttyp und Textproduktion in der deutschen Literatur des Mittelalters*, ed. Elizabeth Andersen, Manfred Eikelmann and Anne Simon, (Trends in Medieval Philology, 7), Berlin and New York: W. de Gruyter, 1–27.

Fujii, Akihiko (2007): *Günther Zainers druckersprachliche Leistung. Untersuchungen zur Augsburger Druckersprache im 15. Jahrhundert*, (Studia Augustana, 15), Tübingen: Niemeyer.

Gärtner, Kurt (2004): Zur Herkunft der Psalmenübersetzung im 'Psalmen kommentar' Heinrichs von Mügeln, in: Plate / Rapp (2004), 97–106.

Geldner, Ferdinand (1968–70), *Die deutschen Inkunabeldrucker*, Stuttgart: Hiersemann.

German STC = *Short Title Catalogue of Books Printed in the German Speaking Countries and German Books Printed in Other Countries from 1455 to 1600 now in the British Museum*, London: British Museum, 1962.

GW = *Gesamtkatalog der Wiegendrucke*, vols 1–8, Leipzig: Harrassowitz, 1940, 2nd revised edn, Stuttgart: Hiersemann, 1968ff.

Hain = Ludwig Hain, *Repertorium bibliographicum in quo libri omnes ab arte typographica inventa usque ad annum MD typis expressi ... recensentur*, Stuttgart and Paris, 1826–38, repr. Milan 1966.

ISTC = Incunabula Short Title Catalogue: www.bl.uk/collections/hoinc.html.

Klapper, Joseph (1938): review of Alfred Bergeler, *Das deutsche Bibelwerk Heinrichs von Mügeln*, Berlin 1938, in Anzeiger für deutsches Altertum, 57: 98–103.

Knapp, Fritz Peter (1999): *Die Literatur des Spätmittelalters in den Ländern Österreich, Steiermark, Kärnten, Salzburg und Tirol von 1273 bis 1439. Erster Halbband: Die Literatur in der Zeit der frühen Habsburger bis zum Tod Albrechts II. 1358 (Geschichte der Literatur in Österreich von den Anfängen bis zur Gegenwart, 2/1)*, Graz: Akad. Druck- und Verlags-Anstalt, 215–233.

Kornrumpf, Gisela (1991): Das 'Klosterneuburger Evangelienwerk' des österreichischen Anonymus, in: Reinitzer (1991), 115–131.

Kornrumpf, Gisela (2004): *Nova et vetera*. Zum Bibelwerk des österreichischen Laien der ersten Hälfte des 14. Jahrhunderts, in: Plate / Rapp ( 2004), 103–121.

Kornrumpf, Gisela: Österreichischer Bibelübersetzer, in: VL², XI, cols 1097–1110.

Kurrelmeyer, W. (1900): 'The Genealogy of the Pre-Lutheran Bibles', *Journal of English and German Philology*, 3: 238–247.

Kurrelmeyer, W. (ed.) (1904–15), *Die erste deutsche Bibel*, 10 vols, Tübingen: Litterarischer Verein in Stuttgart.

Löser, Freimut (1991): Ein zweiter Textzeuge der 'Schlierbacher Bibel'. Zur Laienmissionierung des 14. Jahrhunderts in Österreich, in: Reinitzer (1991), 132–154.

Löser, Freimut (2003): Heinrich von Mügeln und der Psalmenkommentar des 'Österreichischen Bibelübersetzers", in: *Magister et amicus. Festschrift für Kurt Gärtner zum 65. Geburtstag*, ed. Václav Bok and Frank Shaw, Vienna: Edition Praesens, 689–708.

Menhardt, Hermann (1960): *Verzeichnis der altdeutschen literarischen Handschriften der Österreichischen Nationalbibliothek*, I, Berlin:

Akademie Verlag.

Ohly, Friedrich (1958), *Hohelied-Studien: Grundzüge einer Geschichte der Hoheliedauslegung des Abendlandes bis um 1200*, Wiesbaden: Steiner.

Plate, Ralf, and Andrea Rapp (eds) (2004), *Metamorphosen der Bibel, (Vestigia Bibliae*, 24/25 (2002/2003), Bern etc: Peter Lang.

Ratcliffe, F[rederick] W[illiam] (1952): *Enquiry into the vocabulary of the printed versions of Heinrich von Mügeln's Translation of the Psalms*, PhD thesis, University of Manchester.

Ratcliffe, F[rederick] W[illiam] (1961): 'The Psalm translation of Heinrich von Mügeln', *Bulletin of the John Rylands Library*, 43,2: 426–451.

Ratcliffe, F[rederick] W[illiam] (1965a): 'Die Psalmenübersetzung Heinrichs von Mügeln. Die Vorrede, der 'schlichte' Psalmentext und Probleme einer Herausgabe', *Zeitschrift für deutsche Philologie*, 84: 46–76.

Ratcliffe, F[rederick] W[illiam] (1965b): *Edition of Heinrich von Mügeln's Psalm Translation based on the Rein index 204*, 3 vols, Manchester.

Ratcliffe, F[rederick] W[illiam] (1989): *A pre-Lutheran German Psalter: a case study of the fourteenth century translation of Heinrich von Mügeln*, Sanders Readership in Bibliography, 1988–89, [n.pl., 1989] (London BL: Ac 2660.m.).

Reinitzer, Heimo (ed.) (1991): *Deutsche Bibelübersetzungen des Mittelalters, (Vestigia Bibliae*, 9/10 (1987–1988)), Bern etc: Peter Lang

Reske, Christoph (2007): *Die Buchdrucker des 16. und 17. Jahrhunderts im deutschen Sprachgebiet. Auf der Grundlage des gleichnamigen Werkes von Josef Benzing*, (Beiträge zum Buch- und Bibliothekswesen, 51), Wiesbaden: Harrassowitz.

Schmid, Hans-Ulrich (1992): 'Eine spätmittelalterliche Übersetzung des Hohen Liedes' in: *Latein und Volkssprache im deutschen Mittelalter (1100–1500). Regensburger Colloquium 1988*, ed. Nikolaus Henkel and Nigel F. Palmer, Tübingen: Niemeyer, 199–208.

VD16 = *Verzeichnis der im deutschen Sprachbereich erschienenen Drucke des XVI. Jahrhunderts*, 25 vols, Stuttgart: Hiersemann, 1983–2000.

VGT = *Veröffentlichungen der Gesellschaft für Typenkunde des XV. Jahrhunderts*, reprint Osnabrück: O. Zeller, 1966.

VL² = Kurt Ruh et al. (eds): *Die deutsche Literatur des Mittelalters. Verfasserlexikon*. 2nd edn, 14 vols, Berlin and New York: W. de Gruyter, 1983–2008.

Vulgate = *Biblia Sacra iuxta Vulgatam Versionem*, ed. Robertus Weber, 2 vols, Stuttgart: Württembergische Bibelanstalt, 1969.

Widmann, Hans (1965): *Der deutsche Buchhandel in Urkunden und Quellen*. Hamburg: Hauswedell.

Zedler, Gottfried (1931): *Die Handschriften der Nassauischen Landesbibliothek zu Wiesbaden*, (63. Beiheft zum Zentralblatt für Bibliothekswesen), Leipzig: Harrassowitz.

# Ne sint Magistri sine Libris : Early German Printed Books in the Libraries of St Andrews University

*Jeffrey Ashcroft*

## The University Library

On 10 June 1616 King James I & VI issued a letter to the University of St Andrews with thirteen articles of reform to be carried out in this "the Principall fountayne of Religione and good letters in Our native Kingdome". The last two concerned an already vexed matter: "12. That the Librairie be finished with all possible speede, *Ne sint Magistri sine Libris*. 13. That meanes be used to draw schollaris to the New Colledge, for the studdie of Divinitie [...] *Ut non sint Libri sine Magistris*."[1] While St Andrews had never been entirely devoid, since its foundation over the years 1410 to 1413, of any one of three essentials, books, masters and students, it had at times been a close-run thing. During the crisis years before the Reformation an Exhortation in the name of the whole university had described it in 1546 as "sa desolate and destitute bayth of rederris, techarris, and auditouris that it is neir perist and meretis nocht to be callit ane universitie".[2] Archbishop John Hamilton earned congratulation in 1551 for having spared no effort in restoring the "[Academiam] aliquot iam annis bonis libris et professoribus destitutam ac pene desertam."[3]

The full establishment of a university library took two hundred and thirty years, until Alexander Henderson's benefaction of £1,000 in 1642 allowed the "perfyteing" of the "hous appointed for the liberarie", and student fees were diverted from paying for the feasts known as the "bayans [bejants] act", the "weickes" [wakes] and the "poculum" and "bellaria" [wining and dining] to a book purchasing fund.[4] An Arts Faculty resolution in 1415 committed £5 "ad emendum libros textus Aristotelis et commentaria de logica et physica" in Paris, while the same sum was put towards the making of the great Faculty Mace.[5] A common university library to serve the Pedagogy was first mooted by the Faculty in 1456. That led to the construction of a small space at the end of the main lecture hall with a wooden reading desk. Alan Cant, Chancellor and Dean of the Chapel Royal, donated "unum notabilem librum scilicet Magnorum Moralium" (which John Athilmer, Provost of St Salvator's College, promptly removed on long-term loan).[6] This common library, never large, was eclipsed in the sixteenth century, along with the Pedagogy itself, as the colleges of St Salvator (1450), St Leonard (1512) and St Mary (1538), asserted their teaching roles and established libraries of their own.[7]

There is evidence enough that the decline of the university during the years of dissent and violence leading up to the Reformation of 1559 left it seriously short of books.[8] A royal visitation in 1588 found that neither St Salvator's nor St Mary's had proper inventories of their libraries. It has been estimated that in 1600 the total book holdings in the University amounted to no more than around five hundred works, including many duplicates. Vital initiatives then began to come from the royal court. Mary Queen of Scots in 1566 had written a testamentary codicil: "Ie laysse mes liuures qui y sont ceulx en Grec ou Latin a luniuersite de Sintandre pour y commancer une bible", although her will was thwarted by her half-brother, James Stewart, the Regent Moray (who was however himself a major benefactor of St Leonard's College Library). In 1607, Archbishop George Gledstanes persuaded King James to send a Commission of Visitation, whose leading member, George Abbot, soon to become Archbishop of Canterbury, was persuaded of the need for a common library endowed with up-to-date books and urged the matter on the King. It took Gledstanes until 1616 to get James to approve "the dedicatioune of ane commoune Bibliotheque [...] quhairby learning (throche bypast penurie of buikis sumquhat decaying) may be, to the benefit of the kirk and commoune-veil, resuscitat". Abbot himself contributed the first endowment of forty six books. Patrick Young, graduate of St Andrews and royal librarian, gave a further thirteen volumes, and in August 1612 two hundred and twenty eight volumes arrived from the King and his immediate family, "as ane pledge and earnest-penny of his royal munificence [...] out of the gude affection and princelie desire of his Highness' hairt to have ignorance banished, barbarity rooted out, virtue advancit, and gude letters to flourish within his Kingdom of Scotland". However the King did not provide funds for the building, on the site of the old Pedagogy, which was begun in 1612 but not roofed until 1618. Only Alexander Henderson's benefaction in 1642 allowed its fitting out and the "inputing of the bookes".

## Early German printed books

Before the belated establishment of the University Library St Andrews had had libraries for at least four hundred years. Arched recessed book presses from the thirteenth century can still be seen in the east range of the Cathedral cloister.[9] The earliest printed book still in the University's possession, and likely to have been in St Andrews since it was new, dates from c. 1470. My concern in this study is with such printed books that have an early connection with the libraries of the Priory of St Andrew and the colleges of the University, and thus with the stage in the University's book use which precedes central organisation in a common library. The chronological scale of the study, from the mid fifteenth to the mid sixteenth century, is the first hundred years of the printing press. This conveniently coincides with the century between the first evidence of library foundation in the University, in the 1450s, and the Reformation in 1559. My restriction of focus, on books printed in the lands then politically and linguistically German, is more arbitrary. Its justification is the prominence of German printing centres in this one hundred-year period, the need to delimit the material coverable in a short study, and my own research interest in German books.

It must be emphasised at the outset that the books in question are not books in the German language. The oldest examples of printed German now in the University Library are two lower half sheets of an Almanach for the year 1472, used as binder's scrap in a volume of the letters of St Gregory the Great (Augsburg: Gunther Zainer, c.1474), a compilation of devotional texts (Augsburg: Johannes Bämler, 1473), and a German Psalter (Ulm: Johannes Zainer, c.1489).[10] None of these volumes, nor indeed any of the Library's German-language books printed before 1559, were in the collection before the nineteenth century. It would indeed be quite remarkable if the Library had possessed any such early German-language material, given that until the late seventeenth century Latin was the international language of Church and Academe, and that vernacular books in German (the picture is different for Italian, French and English) had little cultural prestige and until the Reformation were often targeted at very local markets.

When we add to these factors the extent to which the survival of any one book or category of books depends on arbitrary and imponderable factors, even in the relatively benign conditions of an academic library, it will be obvious that statistical quantification is not meaningful for such a limited corpus of books. At most it will be possible to confirm conclusions from previous more extensive studies. The emphasis in what follows will therefore be essentially descriptive.

### The Priory of St Andrews and St Leonard's College

The Augustinian Priory of St Andrews was a place of education and learning at the latest by the early thirteenth century, when there is documentary reference to a master of schools and to poor scholars in the burgh. In 1384-1386 James Stewart, son of King Robert II, was "in studio apud Sanctum Andream".[11] The first steps towards the foundation of the University were the initiation in 1410 of a school of higher learning by masters who were mainly Paris graduates, and the grant to them of a charter of incorporation as a "university" by Bishop Henry Wardlaw in 1412. The University was authorised as a *studium generale* and given powers to confer degrees by Pope Benedict XIII in 1413. Thus the University grew out of older educational activities in the Priory.[12] As the faculties of Theology, Canon Law and Arts developed, different centres of gravity emerged. By 1419 the Faculty of Arts had established itself in buildings in South Street, known as the College of St John, which became the *Paedagogium* or Pedagogy, with teaching and residential facilities. Theology was naturally closely linked with the Priory, and this link was retained until its dissolution in 1559, thanks to the foundation in 1512 of St Leonard's College, housed in a former pilgrims' hospice within the monastic precinct, which drew its teaching staff from the canons of the Priory.[13]

Though the medieval library of the Priory is not well documented, and its manuscript holdings did not survive the Reformation in any quantity,[14] the canons were evidently acquiring printed books by 1480 at the latest, and a good number of these are still held in the University Library. An example of books with a Priory provenance is the *Gesta Rhomanorum cum applicationis moralisatis ac misticis* (Strasburg: Grüninger, 1488), inscribed on aii "Liber monasterii Sancti Andree per dominum Jacobum Elioth canonicum eiusdem" [Ill. 1]. Books bought by the Priory were in most cases then assigned to a specified member of the community the community for use in study and teaching, "pro tempore vite", "ex industria", "cuius usu habet", "ex comparatione". On the title-page of this volume a second inscription reads "Liber domini Johannis Duncanson". After the foundation of St Leonard's College in 1512, canons of the Priory engaged in teaching Theology became masters and regents in the College, and books assigned to them seem as a matter of course to have passed by donation or death to the common library. Indeed it appears to be the case that the College Library effectively replaced the Priory Library. Following the example of Prior John Hepburn, co-founder of St Leonard's with Archbishop Alexander Stewart, it seems to have been the convention that principals donated or bequeathed books to the College.[15] Duncanson's name appears with particular frequency. A canon of the Priory, he became Principal c.1556 and was confirmed after the Reformation.

The oldest extant book belonging to a St Andrews theologian, Johannes Duns Scotus, *In quattuor libros sententiarum* (Nuremberg: Koberger, 1481) (parts 2 and 3 of 4), did not come to St Leonard's directly from the Priory. It is inscribed on folio 2$^r$ of part 2: "Liber Johannis Doless" and "Nunc autem ex dono eiusdem spectans ad communem bibliothecam Collegii Sancti Leonardi". Dolass (there are seven variant spellings of his name) is named over fifty times in the Acta of the Faculty of Arts between 1455 and 1498; he served the Faculty in a variety of posts, including Bursar and Dean.[16] When admitted *ad lecturam* in 1458, and again in 1466-1469, Magister Johannes Dolass "chose his books" – for his use in lectures, and presumably, where necessary, to be purchased by the Faculty. He was not a canon, but a student, then *magister* and *licentiatus in theologia* (1485-86) in the Pedagogy of the Faculty of Arts. He is assumed to have died c.1500, but that is at variance with the statement that this book was transferred "by his gift" to St Leonard's, which was not founded until 1512. What both these first two sample volumes have in common, however, is that their bindings are both possibly the work of fifteenth-century St Andrews workshops.

Otherwise printed books which arrived in St Andrews before 1500 seem in the large majority to have come first to the Priory, and "most, if not all, surviving books from the cathedral priory passed through the library of St Leonard's."[17] Among the two surviving volumes donated to the College by its founder, Prior Hepburn, is Pope Gregory the Great's *Moralia in Job*, printed in Paris in 1495 by the German printers, Ulrich Gering and Berthold Rembolt, brought to the Sorbonne in 1470 as

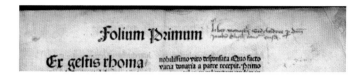

Ill. 1: *Gesta Rhomanorum*, Strasburg, 1488 sig. a2 recto
User's mark in top margin

Ill. 2: Peter Lombard, *Liber sententiarum*, Nuremberg, 1481
Front cover of binding

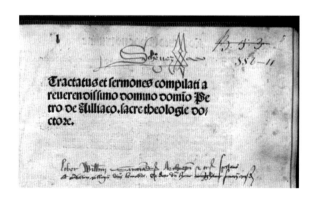

Ill. 3: Petrus de Ailliaco, *Tractatus et Sermones*, Strasburg, 1490.
Schevez inscription.

publishers to the University of Paris. Another Franco-German imprint is Bonaventura, *Super quattuor sententiarum libros* (Lyons: Jacques Sacon for Johannes Koberger, 1515). The Nuremberg publishing house of Koberger used the Lyons press to provide additional printing capacity and to give easier access to markets in western parts of Europe.[18] Of the two early copies in St Andrews one is marked "Liber monasterii Sanctiandree datus per alexandrum zwng [i.e. Young]" and then "et a collegio sancti leonardi" in the handwriting of John Annand. Young studied at St Salvator's College and graduated bachelor in theology in 1492, before entering the Priory.[19] He became Principal of St Leonard's in 1540. Annand was Principal from 1544 to 1549; a staunch conservative in the pre-Reformation controversies, he taught both theology and canon law, and adjudicated in a trial for heresy in 1541. The second copy is inscribed "Ex libris domini Johannis guidfallowe Canonici Sanctiandree" - John Goodfellow is recorded in 1541. It has no St Leonard's mark and belonged in the later sixteenth and early seventeenth century to Robert Pont (1524-1606) and his son-in-law Charles Lumsden (matriculated 1579, d. 1630). Augustine, *De civitate Dei* (Basel: Johann Amerbach, 1489), has the ex libris device "R. gracia dei mecum. H" of Canon Robert Hyndmers or Hindmarsh, who died c. 1500; marginal notes in the volume show that it too was later used by John Annand.

### Archbishop William Schevez

As well as those volumes which document the role of the Priory and its canons in book purchase and use, the University Library possesses the major part of the most important personal book collection extant from fifteenth-century Scotland. William Schevez, from the village of Sheves, near Ellon in Aberdeenshire, graduated as *magister* in the Faculty of Arts on 7 June 1456.[20] He also studied in Louvain at times between 1457 and 1470. By 1471 he was physician to King James III and was nominated as Archdeacon of St Andrews in 1474. Archbishop Patrick Graham refused to admit him to office, but in 1477 Graham was deposed for simony and blasphemy and Schevez became Archbishop and Primate of Scotland in 1478. Though judgements vary on his character and political role, Schevez was certainly a remarkable bibliophile. Jasper Laet of Borchloen dedicated his book *De Eclipsi Solis anni MCCCCXCI currentis Pronosticum* in 1491 to "the most reverend father and lord in Christ, William, Archbishop of St Andrews, Primate of the whole Kingdom of Scotland", and makes the large claim that "In St Andrews, where there is an illustrious University and a host of learned men, although you give freely in all ways, you have especially devoted yourself to the provision of most valuable libraries, filled with books of every kind." There is no evidence that Schevez set up libraries other than his own personal collection, but this must have been for its time a substantial one. Twenty-eight printed books and eleven manuscripts are known to be extant.[21] Of the printed books, thirteen are in St Andrews University Library. Six of these are from German presses, six from the Netherlands, and one from Italy. It was most probably from Louvain that Schevez obtained much of his library, and a number of the St Andrews volumes have Louvain, Bruges or Ghent bindings. All the German printing centres represented – Cologne, Strasburg, Basel and Nuremberg - have easy river connection with the Netherlands, and St Andrews had strong academic links with Louvain in the fifteenth century.[22] Giles of Assisi, *Aurea verba de gratia Dei* (Cologne: Ulrich Zell, c. 1470), is the oldest German printed book known to have reached St Andrews. It may have been an early purchase by Schevez or bought second-hand, given that only one other of Schevez's books dates from before 1480, and that the *Aurea verba* is bound together with five other works printed in Louvain and Brussels in the 1480s, in a binding probably made for Schevez in Louvain. Other volumes with Louvain bindings are Peter Lombard, *Liber sententiarum* (Nuremberg: Koberger, 1481) [Ill. 2], St John Chrysostom, *Homiliae super Matthaeum and Sermones notabiles* (Cologne: Johann Koelhoff, 1487), and Cassiodorus, *Expositio in Psalterium* (Basel: Johann Amerbach, 1491). Characteristic of the bindings made for Schevez, in calf over oak boards, are fine blind-tooled stamps with motifs such as fleur-de-lys, pelican and double-headed eagle, and horn windows with hand-written titles on the front board. The Chrysostom binding has the bird and bow rebus of the binder John Ravescot. This volume is marked "Scheuez" on the title page, on fol. a1 and on the verso of the final leaf, where it is also inscribed "Nunc liber domini Johannis Symsone". Symson was a canon of the Priory at the end of the fifteenth century. On the front pastedown is the bookplate of William Gott of Wyther Grange, Yorkshire (1797-1863). Otherwise all the German prints in St Andrews passed from Schevez's possession to St Leonard's College. Pierre d'Ailly, *Tractatus et sermones* (Strasburg: [Printer of the 1483 Jordanus], 1490), has Schevez's signature, then the inscription "spectans ad bibliothecam collegii diui Leonardi [Ill. 3]. Ex dono domini thome cunynghame primarii eiusdem" (Cunningham became Principal in 1537). Peter Lombard's *Sententiae* and Alberto Trotti, *De horis canonicis* (Louvain: Johannes of Westphalia, 1485), show, added to Schevez's signature, the ownership mark of John Duncanson.

While a number of Schevez's books were evidently absorbed into St Leonard's College Library from c.1500, it does not appear that they were used by canons in their study and teaching until after the Archbishop's death in 1497. Two final examples of books which probably came from the Cathedral Priory, but whose route of transmission is not documented, are Albrecht von Eyb, *Margarita poetica* (Strasburg: [Printer of the 1483 Vitas Patrum], c.1483-1484), with a contemporary binding probably carried out in St Andrews, and Jordan of Quedlinburg, *Postillae de tempore* (Strasburg: [Printer of the 1483 Jordanus], 1483), also with a fine binding, perhaps by J. Guilebert of Bruges. Both of these books have only the inscriptions "Liber/Codex domini Johannis Duncansoun". It is interesting that both fall into the same period of the 1480s as the bulk of Schevez's books, and that they have bindings comparable with Schevez's commissions rather than with the general run of books inherited by St Leonard's from the Priory. It is not likely that either of them was purchased by or for Duncanson (who cannot have been active much before 1530). While neither bears evidence of Schevez's ownership, it is not impossible that they were acquired for the Priory in conjunction with acquisitions of his in the Netherlands. [23]

## Reformation and Humanism up to 1559

St Leonard's College was founded in 1512 by Prior John Hepburn with the support of Archbishop Alexander Stewart, as the *Collegium pauperum clericorum ecclesie Sanctiandree*, intended to ensure the recruitment of well educated young men for the priesthood and the Priory, and "to steady the tossing barque of St Peter".[24] Alexander Stewart, born c. 1493 as the illegitimate son of King James IV, was named Archbishop *in commendam* at the age of eleven. He was sent to Padua in 1508 to read law. In addition he studied logic and rhetoric with Erasmus as his tutor, who praised his character and intellect in the *Adagia* and accompanied him on a grand tour to Siena, Rome and Naples.[25] On his return to Scotland he showed interest in reforming the Pedagogy. On 9 September 1513 he fell with his father at the battle of Flodden. What the young Erasmian might have accomplished for his College and its Library one can only speculate, but certainly their access to humanist learning was delayed for half a century. Nor is the impact of the Lutheran or the early Swiss Reformation discernible in the early book holding of the University in the 1520s or 1530s, despite the evidence of Lutheran opinions in St Leonard's College during the principalship of Gavin Logie from 1523 to 1534, when "Yee have drunken of Sanct Leonard's well"[26] became a metaphor for harbouring Protestant sympathies. When Patrick Hamilton came back from a year of study in Wittenberg in 1527, he may have brought Lutheran books with him, but if so, they were most likely burnt with him at the stake in front of St Salvator's in February 1528. Alexander Alane or Alesius left to avoid martyrdom and became a leading figure in Protestant Germany. Gilbert Winram, who was a student at St Leonard's, graduating M.A. in 1521, also left for Germany and died in Marburg c.1530. His signature appears on the title page of one of the University Library's two copies of Erasmus, *Novum Testamentum omne* (Basel: Froben, 1522). There is no evidence that it was in the College Library or of its further transmission. Another work of Erasmus, the *Paraphrasis in Evangelium Johannis apostoli* (Basel: Froben, 1523), was in the College Library. It has the signature of Thomas Cunningham, but as canon of the Priory, and must have been in the College before Cunningham became Principal in 1534.[27] Dominant in St Andrews in these years, however, were the conservative figures of John Major of St Salvator's, "last of the schoolmen", and John Annand of St Leonard's (described by John Knox as "a rottin papist"). Both had roles in the heresy trials which scarred the history of the University from 1539 to 1558.[28]

There is a dearth of German books which can be assigned to St Leonard's after 1510, and in particular of Reformation titles. German presses were printing little apart from Reformation material from 1520 onwards, and militant orthodoxy prevailed in Priory and University. Of ten German books which bear the *ex libris* inscriptions of John Duncanson seven date from before 1507, so that Duncanson can have had no hand in their purchase. His signature merely registers their possession by St Leonard's. The remaining three comprise works by the Reformers Heinrich Bullinger (Zurich, 1554 and 1557) and Johann Brenz (Frankfurt, 1545), and Duncanson presumably acquired these after he himself subscribed to the Reformation in 1559. The picture is the same for his eight French imprints, of which six were published before or in 1510, with a volume on Conciliar reform (1547) and a work by Jean Calvin (Geneva, 1552) evidently belonging to Duncanson's Protestant conversion. Lack of money in the modestly endowed College, as well as the growing religious ferment and violence in St Andrews from c.1530, clearly inhibited the growth of the book stock. What appears to be the first work of Martin Luther to enter the St Leonard's Library arrived as late as 1588, when William Christison donated a massively bound volume containing the four parts of the *Enarrationes in Genesin* (Nuremberg: Johannes vom Berg, 1550-1554). The binding is dated 1555. The first pastedown has Christison's *ex libris*: "Willelmus Joannis cognomento Christisonn nacione Scotus apud Bergenses verbi divini minister". On his return from exile in Bergen he became minister in Dundee.[29]

Archbishop Alexander Stewart had intended a reform of the Pedagogy in 1509-1511 and his project was revived by Archbishop James Beaton in 1525, when he petitioned Rome for permission to set up a College of St Mary on the same site. The Papal Bull was not forthcoming until 1538. The "New College" was primarily meant to train candidates for the secular priesthood, thus complementing St Leonard's mission to staff the Priory, and to teach Canon Law. Beaton's cousin, Archibald Hay (briefly Provost of St Mary's in 1546-1547), greeted the foundation with a *Panegyricus* envisaging it as a fusion of theology and humanist sacred philology, a Trilingual College on the model of the Collège de France founded in Paris in 1530.[30] Yet even in this ambitious venture there is no evidence for the provision of an adequate library. The earliest inventories show that neither before nor after 1559 was there any concerted effort to acquire a library consistent with Beaton's, let alone with Hay's, objectives. To the extent that the humanist vision was realised before 1559 the credit seems to belong to the St Andrews Blackfriars, notably to Friar John Grierson, provincial prior of the Dominican Order in Scotland from 1523 to his death in 1564.[31] A full convent in St Andrews was not established until 1516. Grierson made it his residence from 1525, and after the foundation of St Mary's

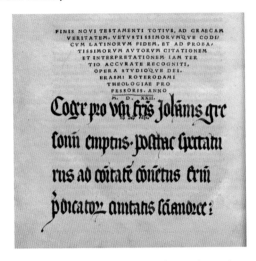

Ill. 4: Erasmus, *Novum Testamentum*, Basel 1522 (copy 1)
Colophon and inscription by John Grierson

Ill. 5: Ptolemy, *Geographica*, Lyons 1541. Title page

College members of the Dominican house provided theological teaching. Grierson is recorded as Professor of Holy Scripture in 1549 and as Dean of Theology from 1553. He recanted before the St Andrews Presbytery in 1560 but continued to act as Provincial in order to effect the disposal of the Order's property. The Dominican house provided theological teaching. In 1522 he drew up a booklist of one hundred volumes in the Friary library.[32] This inventory does not include the copy of Erasmus, *Novum Testamentum omne* (Basel: Froben, 1522), which survives in the University Library and has the inscription on A2r and E8v: "Codex pro vsu fratris Johannis gresoun emptus. posthac spectans ad communitatem conuentus fratrum predicatorum ciuitatis sanctiandree"[Ill. 4]. It is tempting to imagine the book being used in St Mary's College, but there is no evidence for that. A copy (also Froben, 1522) of Erasmus's companion volume of *Annotationes* to the Greek and Latin New Testament texts does appear in Grierson's list (now in St Peter's College, Cardross). Grierson's list includes further works by Erasmus, including the *Enchiridion militis christiani*.

### Post-Reformation German books

The process of reshaping the University into a Reformed Protestant institution was long and faltering, through the *First Book of Discipline*, the parliamentary committee of 1563 which provoked George Buchanan's "Opinion anent the Reformation of the Universitie of St Andrews", the commission of the Regent Morton (1574), the "New Foundation" of 1579, and royal visitations in 1597 and 1599.[33] As we have seen, the creation of a University Library had to wait until 1608 and even then took until 1642 to result in a functioning building and accessible book collection. However major donations, that of the Regent Moray to St Leonard's College, the royal Foundation Gift, and the bequest of William Guild, claim final attention to the extent that they brought further German books published before 1559 into the University's libraries at still relatively early dates.

The Stewart kings' habit of producing bastard sons, and providing for them by appointing them to ecclesiastical preferments, brought further benefit to St Andrews when in 1538 James V made his seven-year-old son James Stewart Prior *in commendam* of St Andrews.[34] In 1547 he matriculated in St Leonard's. James was evacuated to France with Princess Mary during the disastrous events which stemmed from George Wishart's martyrdom in 1546 - the assassination of Cardinal David Beaton, the French siege of the episcopal castle, and the English invasion of Fife. He may have studied with Petrus Ramus in Paris. He returned to St Andrews in 1548 and began to play a political part in the last years before the Reformation. In 1558 he went back to France to negotiate Mary's marriage with the Dauphin. He used his title as Commendator of the Priory up to 1561. On Mary's return to Scotland as Queen she made him Earl of Moray. For all his short academic career, and his onerous years as Regent until his assassination in 1570, he amassed a remarkable scholarly

library, much of which came to St Leonard's. The donation happened in
two stages. Books gifted before c.1560 have inscriptions identifying him
as *commendator prioratus filius illustrissimi principis Jacobi quintii Scotorum
regis*, while the later bequest is in the name of *Iacobus Steuard C.P.S.*, with
his motto *Salus per XPM*, and these volumes have the sumptuous armorial
bindings of the Regent of Scotland. Among earlier German imprints in
the first donation are two mathematical works: Johann Schoener, *Opera
mathematica* (Nuremberg: Johann vom Berg & Ulrich Neuber, 1551), and
the *Opera omnia* of Ptolemy, edited by Erasmus Oswald Schreckenfuchs
(Basel: Heinrich Petri, 1551). This mathematical theme was reinforced
by George Buchanan, who became Principal of St Leonard's in 1566,
with his own donations of Johannes Müller (Regiomontanus), *Tabulae*
(Tübingen: Ulrich Morhart, 1550), and Michael Stifel, *Arithmetica integra*
(Nuremberg, Johann Petreius, 1544). Moray's later donation includes
Sebastian Münster's *Cosmographia* (Basel: Heinrich Petri, 1550). However
its principal value lies in the large collection of the magisterial editions
of the Church Fathers and of Classical Latin authors edited by Erasmus
and printed by Froben in Basel. Examples are the ten-volume works of
Saint Augustine (1528-1529) and the five-volume edition of St Ambrose
(1538), Pliny the Elder's *Historia mundi* (1549), and Suetonius's *Vitae
Caesarum* (1546).

The Regent Moray's library gave a notable boost to the resources of the
University in a wide range of aspects of humanism. A smaller reinforcement
of the Erasmian editions and of Reformation writings came from Moray's
half-brother, Robert Stewart, Bishop of Caithness, who matriculated in St
Leonard's in 1550. Of sixteen volumes donated by him twelve are from
German printing houses. Erasmus is again prominent with Froben imprints
of the *Adagia* (1546), the *Annotationes in Novum Testamentum* (1540),
and editions of Hilary of Poitiers, *Lucubrationes* (1535) and Josephus, *De
bello iudaico* (1548). Other Basel patristic editions are Beatus Rhenanus's
*Tertullian* (Froben, 1550), Augustine's *Commentaries on the Old and New
Testaments*, ed. by Johann Gast (Herwagen, 1542), and St Basil the Great,
*Opera* (Herwagen, 1540). There are also two works by Melanchthon, both
commentaries on Paul's Epistle to the Romans (Wittenberg: Joseph Clug,
1530, and Marburg: Franciscus Rhodus, 1532), and Johann Bugenhagen's
*Interpretatio Psalmorum* (Basel: Adam Petri, 1524). Caithness's books, like
Moray's, mostly have his own regal, monogrammed calf binding.

While a main value of these post-Reformation Stewart bequests was to
repair the dearth of works of humanist sacred philology and Renaissance
classicism in the St Andrews libraries, the Foundation Gift of 1611-1612
was, it appears, deliberately planned by George Abbot and Patrick Young
to concentrate on recent and contemporary material.[35] James I & VI's
message, sent with the main consignment of volumes in August 1612,
promised indeed that the flow of books would be "continued yearly to such
time as the Library of the University comes to some reasonable perfection."

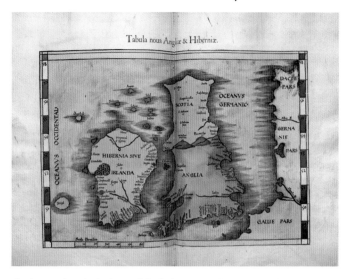

Ill. 6: Map "Anglia/Hibernia" (Tabula Nova 29)

Sadly this promise, like the funding of the Library building, was soon forgotten. The book lists compiled at the time show that the Foundation Gift totalled two hundred and twenty eight volumes, priced at £267 14s. 10d. The small part of the Gift that falls within our category of German imprints up to 1559 can be briefly illustrated with three unusual examples. Peter Young, brother of Patrick and likewise a graduate of St Leonard's, gave a Latin Koran, published in Basel by Johannes Oporinus in 1543 (three volumes bound in one), with copious supporting texts and annotation by Theodor Bibliander and Philipp Melanchthon. This Young specifically designated for the St Leonard's Library. Among George Abbot's donation is an incunable, Angelus Carletus, *Summa angelica de casibus conscientiae* (Strasburg: Martin Flach, 1491), rebound in archiepiscopal gold-tooled calf, while Patrick Young contributed Duns Scotus, *Quaestiones in quattuor libros Sententiarum* (Nuremberg: Koberger, 1481), bound in Koberger's workshop, earlier owned by John Adamson, possibly the graduand in the Pedagogy recorded in 1498.

**Pro captu lectoris habent sua fata libelli**
William Guild (1586-1657) left substantial legacies of books to the University of St Andrews and the University of Edinburgh, having revoked his original bequest to the University of Aberdeen, of which he had been Principal.[36] St Andrews possesses ninety-eight of them on a very wide range of subjects. The quite ample evidence of their previous ownership suggests that Guild busily bought up books from other private libraries in the first half of the seventeenth century. In particular thirty-one of the St

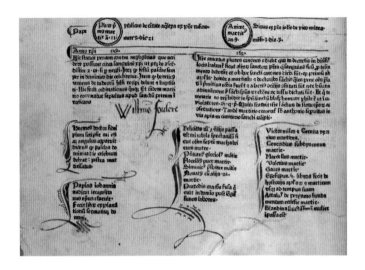

Ill. 7: Werner Rolevinck, *Fasciculus temporum*, Cologne, 1478.
Fol. 39ᵛ

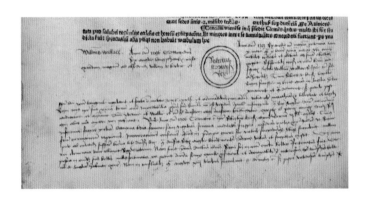

Ill. 8: Werner Rolevinck, *Fasciculus temporum*, Cologne, 1478.
Fol. 69ᵛ

Andrews books had earlier been in the hands of Sir Thomas Henryson, Lord Chesters, who died in 1638. Two of the books Guild donated, which came to Scotland very soon after they were printed, preserve unusually interesting evidence of their Scottish ownership and use.

In 1541 the Lyons printer, Gaspard Trechsel, produced for the Vienne publisher, Hugues la Porte, a new edition of Ptolemy's *Geographica* [Ill. 5]. It was based on Willibald Pirckheimer's Latin translation of the Greek text, and re-used the same fifty maps, first made by Martin Waldseemüller for Lorenz Fries, which appear in Pirckheimer's edition, published by Johann Grüninger, Strasburg, 1525 [Ill. 6].[37] Guild's copy in the St Andrews University Library has on its title page the inscriptions of five successive owners who register with unusual precision the links between them. The sequence begins: "Ex libris Ro[berti] Danyelston. Rector[is] a[d] Dysert et amico[rum]." There is no date, but we can place the entry between the book's publication in 1541 and the following entry dated 1548. Danielston is recorded as matriculating in St Leonard's College in 1535.[38] By the 1540s he was parish priest of Dysart, a small port next to Kirkcaldy. He possessed the Ptolemy text as a member of a group of friends. Books, especially ones illustrated with high-quality maps, expertly hand-coloured in this copy, were expensive, and shared ownership by a syndicate is a rational arrangement. Danielston evidently had humanist interests well outside his theological education and vocation. Here is a young graduate who has gained access to secular humanist culture at the height of Reformation upheaval, at a time when St Leonard's College had nothing comparable in its library. By 1548 the Ptolemy edition has passed on to another member of the *sodalitas* who adds his *ex libris*: "Spe expecto J. Steinstonij et amicorum". John Steinston may be the student of that name who matriculated in St Leonard's in 1520 and graduated M.A. in St Andrews in 1524. On a2$^r$ and h5$^v$ he identifies himself as Precentor of Glasgow Cathedral and Protonotary Apostolic. In 1552 he was Rector of Glasgow University.[39] The next link in the chain of bibliophile friends is undated: "Nunc Eduardi Henrysonis quod fuit ex amicis Jhoannis Steinstoun". From Edward Henryson the book passed to his son: "Thomas Henryson ex dono patri suo charissimi possidet" and "Ex libris magistri Thome henrysoun Aduocati 1592".[40] Edward Henryson (1522-c.1590) studied law in Paris and Bourges, where he became professor of Roman Law in1553. From 1556 he taught law, Greek and Latin in Edinburgh. His son, Thomas Henryson (d. 1638), was an advocate in Edinburgh, then judge in the Court of Session, taking the title Lord Chesters. Finally comes Guild's customary inscription: "Liber Gulielmi Guild S.T.D." Over a span of more than a century, then, Ptolemy's *Geographica* had - initially, at least - intellectual interest, then presumably bibliophile and antiquarian value, for owners before and after 1559.

Guild's bequest includes a much earlier work, similarly combining scholarly and aesthetic appeal, which came to Scotland most likely when new, and whose ownership and use can also be reconstructed in part. The *Fasciculus temporum* (Cologne: Nicolas Gotz, 1478) by Werner Rolevinck, monk in the Carthusian priory in Cologne, belonged to William Fouler, Dean of Haddington from 1465 to 1487.[41] It is inscribed "Liber magistri W. Fouler" on xxiv$^v$, with his initials on xxvii$^v$, and "Willelmus Foulere" on xxix$^v$ and xxxviii$^v$ [Ill. 7]. Rolevinck (1425-1502), a Westphalian peasant's son, was a moral theologian linked with the *devotio moderna*. He also corresponded with the humanist, Johannes Trithemius.[42] Progressive and proto-humanistic in his theology, Rolevinck's historiography is essentially traditional. The *Fasciculus temporum* is constructed on the template of the medieval universal history, but its typographical design and layout is innovative. Into the historical narrative Rolevinck introduces a strand of reference to the foundation of cities in ancient and medieval times. Both these innovations are taken up and developed by Hartmann Schedel in his *Liber chronicarum* (Nuremberg: Koberger, 1493), (the so-called "Nuremberg Chronicle"). Fouler's interest in the *Fasciculus temporum* extended at the very least to careful rubrication of the text – his signature shows his calligraphic ability, though he bought the book probably with the woodcuts already coloured, and certainly already bound.

The volume re-emerges into historical record in 1593, when Alexander Fraser wrote his name at the head of the index ("Tabula brevis", fol. 67-74, but bound in before the text in this copy). Along with it is the *ex libris* "Liber magistri Johannis Leslie". Both have been partly obliterated, perhaps by William Guild who has entered his own name at this point too. John Leslie (1527-1596) was educated at Aberdeen University, became a canon of Aberdeen Cathedral in 1547 and Professor of Canon Law at Aberdeen University in 1562.[43] He had studied in France and graduated doctor of law in Paris. After 1589 he remained staunchly Roman Catholic and a champion of Mary Queen of Scots. During her English exile he acted as her advisor and envoy. Accused of complicity in the Ridolfi plot, he was sent to the Tower, then exiled in 1574. The years from 1575 until his death were spent in Rome and France. Alexander Fraser was possibly his amanuensis, and it may have been he who systematically used the bottom margins of the *Fasciculus temporum* to enter a chronological supplement of Scottish history, excerpted from sixteenth-century sources. He perceptively adopts layout devices modelled on Rolevinck's in order to structure his narrative of medieval Scotland [Ill. 8]. Why and where this was done is unclear, equally whether it has any connection with John Leslie's own history of Scotland from 1057, *De origine, moribus et rebus gestis Scotorum* (Rome: in aedibus populi Romani, 1578), or his vernacular *History of Scotland* from James II to James V (1570), a continuation of Hector Boece's *Scotorum historia* (1527).

There is related evidence for the reception of the *Fasciculus temporum* in Scotland. It is listed, for instance, by John Grierson in his 1522 catalogue of Dominican books. More interestingly Gilbert Haldane (or

Hawding), recorded as a student in the Arts Faculty in St Andrews in 1478, bought his copy of the *Fasciculus* in Louvain in 1491, and "finding it defective in Scottish history, supplied the want by interleaving it with a Scots chronicle".[44] It is now in Edinburgh University Library. That this kind of supplementation was a not uncommon procedure is suggested by the copy of Hartmann Schedel's *Liber chronicarum* bought in 1495 for the Worshipful Company of Drapers in London, in which marginal entries connect the narrative with events in English history, expanding for instance Schedel's account of King Arthur on fol. 143$^v$. Where Schedel leaves blank leaves (259$^r$ -262$^v$) before his account of the Apocalypse, for readers to add stop-press notes on events after 1493, lists of Lord Mayors and Sheriffs of London since 1189 have been entered.[45]

Though the accretion and survival of fifteenth- and sixteenth-century books in St Andrews libraries is subject to imponderable historical forces, local circumstances and random chance, an examination even of a segment of bibliographical evidence is revealing, at the very least, of the quantitative significance of German printing in its first hundred years and of its reception in the particular intellectual and cultural contexts of late medieval and early modern Scotland.[46]

## Notes

1  G.H. Bushnell, "The Early History of the Library of St Andrews University", in: *Henderson's benefaction. A tercentenary acknowledgement of the University's debt to Alexander Henderson*, ed. J.B. Salmond & G.H. Bushnell (St Andrews University Publications 2), St Andrews, 1942, 41-48 (43).

2  Ronald G. Cant, *The University of St Andrews: a Short history*, Edinburgh, 1970, 36.

3  Annie I. Dunlop, *Acta Facultatis Artium Universitatis Sanctiandree 1413-1588* (St Andrews University Publications 61), Edinburgh, 1964, lxii, note 7.

4  Bushnell, "Early History", 47.

5  Dunlop, *Acta*, 6.

6  Ibid., xxvi and 114-115.

7  On the medieval colleges of St Andrews in general see Cant, *The University*, 23-41. Ibid., *The College of St Salvator* (St Andrews University Publications 47), Edinburgh, 1950; John Herkless & Robert Kerr Hannay, *The College of St Leonard*, Edinburgh 1905; Bushnell, "Early History", passim.; John Higgitt, *Scottish libraries* (Corpus of British Medieval Library Catalogues 12), London, 2006), xlii-xlv, 257-366; John Durkan, "The Library of St Salvator's College, St Andrews", *The Bibliothek*, 2/3, 1959-62, Part 3, 97-100.

8  The following is based on Bushnell, *Early History*, 34-48.

9  John Gifford, *The Buildings of Scotland*: Fife, London, 1988, 366. A

fourteenth-century Priory *ex libris* reads "Liber de communi armariolo S Andr". See Bushnell, "Early History", 24-27, and Higgitt, *Scottish libraries*, xlviii. Nothing remains of the stone library building built by Prior David Ramsay in the 1460s.

10 I have not supplied shelf-marks for the volumes cited in this study. Full descriptive catalogue details are readily accessible online from the St Andrews University electronic catalogue (SAULCAT) on www.http://library.st-andrews.ac.uk . On the German Psalter, Ulm, c.1489, see Jeffrey Ashcroft, "Bruder Hans's 'Teutsch Psalter'. Uses of literacy in a late medieval monastery", *Gutenberg-Jahrbuch*, 60, 1985, 125-139.

11 Higgitt, *Scottish libraries*, 375.

12 Cant, *The University*, 3-6.

13 Ibid., 29-32.

14 Archbishop John Spottiswoode reported in 1560 that when the citizens of St Andrews stormed the Priory in 1559 the "Registers of the Church and Bibliotheques [were] cast into the fire". Higgitt, *Scottish Libraries*, lix.

15 On the beginnings of St Leonard's College Library, see Bushnell, "Early History", 31-32.

16 Dunlop, *Acta*, Index: "Dolass, John", and J. Maitland Anderson, *Early Records of the University of St Andrews. The Graduation Roll 1413-1579. The Matriculation Roll 1473-1579* (Publications of the Scottish Historical Society, 3rd series, Vol. 8), Edinburgh, 1926, 34 & 36.

17 Higgitt, *Scottish libraries*, 234.

18 See Johannes Pommeranz, "Fernando Colón's Buchkäufe in Nürnberg im Winter 1521-22. Zum Vertrieb des Nürnberger Buchhandels im Zeitalter der Fugger", in: *Quasi Centrum Europae. Europa kauft in Nürnberg*, ed. Hermann Maué et al., (Exhibition Catalogue, Germanisches Nationalmuseum), Nuremberg, 2002, 305-319 (310-311).

19 For the documentation of this and other students in St Andrews see Dunlop, Acta, passim.; Maitland Anderson, *Early Records*, for Young, 81, 85, 190, 294.

20 George H. Bushnell, "Portrait of a bibliophile IV: William Schevez, Archbishop of St Andrews, d. 1497", in: *The Book Collector*, 9, 1960, 19-29; Dunlop, *Acta*, xxxii-xxxix. An abusively Protestant picture of Schevez is painted by John Herkless & Robert Kerr Hannay, *Archbishops of St Andrews* I, Edinburgh, 1907, 152-153: "[...] a scheming, time-serving prelate who gained ascendancy over James III by astrological quackery. [...] The love of books is almost the one noble feature [...] in the meagre catalogue of the virtues and vices of this prelate, who had not the mind of Anselm or Becket but had the heart of a menial".

21 John Durkan & Anthony Ross, *Early Scottish libraries*, Glasgow, 1961, 47-49; John Durkan & R.V. Pringle, "St Andrews Additions to Durkan & Ross: Some unrecorded Scottish Pre-Reformation ownership

inscriptions in St Andrews University Library", in: *The Bibliothek*, 9, 1978-79, 13-20 (14); John Durkan, "Further Additions to Durkan & Ross: Some newly discovered Scottish Pre-Reformation provenances", in: *The Bibliothek*, 10, 1980-81, 87-98. Geoffrey Hargreaves, formerly Keeper of Rare Books in St Andrews University Library, has entered a definitive list of Schevez's extant books at the end of the Library's reference copy of Bushnell's article on Schevez.

22  Margaret Lane Ford, "Importation of printed books into England and Scotland", in: *The Cambridge History of the Book in Britain*, ed. Lotte Hellinga & J.B. Trapp, Cambridge, 1999, Vol. I, 179-201 (194-195).

23  Higgitt, *Scottish libraries*, 236, suggests that Schevez "acquired [his books] for himself rather than for the community."

24  See Cant, *The University*, 28-33.

25  Note also Erasmus's letter to Willibald Pirckheimer, 14 March 1525, describing the ring which was Alexander's parting gift to Erasmus: *Willibald Pirckheimers Briefwechsel*, Vol. V, ed. Helga Scheible, Munich, 2001, no. 914, 337-350. Erasmus, *Letters, January-December 1525*, transl. Alexander Dalzell, annotated Charles G. Nauert jr. (The Collected Works of Erasmus 11), Toronto 1994, number 1558, 65-75.

26  Gavin Logie, Principal of St Leonard's from 1523 until 1534, was an early Lutheran sympathiser and according to Calderwood (*Historie of the Kirk of Scotland*, Vol. 1, 82-83) "instilled into his scholars the truthe secretlie, which they, in processe of time, spread through the whole countrie, whereupon did arise a proverb, 'Yee have drunken of Sanct Leonards well.'" (Quoted by Bushnell, "Early History", 32).

27  However it also has, crossed through, the inscription of "Johannes hamylton". Archbishop Hamilton otherwise donated books to St Mary's College, which he re-founded in 1552-1554.

28  Dunlop, *Acta*, l-lxiii.

29  Maitland Anderson, *Early Records*, 210; Durkan & Pringle, *St Andrews Additions*, 15. The University Library also has Christison's copy of a 1553 edition of the Great Bible. He also gave volumes of Augustine to the Dundee burgh library. See Durkan, "The Libraries of sixteenth-century Scotland", in Higgitt, *Scottish libraries*, lxxi. In following centuries many older German books came to St Andrews University Library from Scottish manses. An early example is the collection of William Moore, minister of Dunino (1663-1664) and of Holy Trinity, St Andrews (1664-1684), who left one hundred and eighty three volumes to St Salvator's College. See W.E.K. Rankin, "A seventeenth-century manse library", *Records of the Scottish Church History Society*, 17, 1972, 43—63.

30  J.K. Cameron, "A Trilingual College For Scotland: The Founding of St Mary's College" in : *In Divers Manners. A St Mary's Miscellany*, ed. D. W. D. Shaw, St Andrews, 1990, 29-42.

31  W. Moir Bryce, "The Black Friars and the Scottish universities", *Scottish Historical Review*, 9, 1911, 1-9; Higgitt, *Scottish Libraries*, 238-256. John Durkan, "The cultural background in sixteenth-century Scotland" in: *Essays on the Scottish Reformation 1513-1625*, ed. David McRoberts, Glasgow, 1962, 274-331, suggests that under Grierson as Dean of Theology "the St Mary's set-up [...] was largely Dominican" (325). See also John Durkan, "The beginnings of humanism in Scotland", *Innes Review*, 4, 1953, 5-24.

32  Higgitt, *Scottish libraries*, 240-256. See also John Durkan & Julian Russell, "John Grierson's book-list", *Innes Review*, 28, 1977, 39-49.

33  Cant, *The University*, 45-66.

34  For the following see D.W. Doughty, "The library of James Stewart, Earl of Moray, 1531-1570", *Innes Review*, 21, 1970, 17-29; Bushnell, "Early History", 35.

35  For this and the following see Bushnell, Early History, 37-41. The inventory of books is printed in *The Miscellany of the Maitland Club*, Edinburgh, 1834, 322-329. See R.V. Pringle, *A revised transcript, with annotations, of the "Foundation List" of 1612-13* (St Andrews University Library, Sources for Library History 1), St Andrews, 1976.

36  *Oxford Dictionary of National Biography*, ed. H.C.G. Matthew & Brian Harrison, Oxford, 2004, Vol. 24, 185-186.

37  Gaspard (or Caspar) Trechsel was the son of Johann Trechsel, a graduate of Erfurt University who emigrated to France before 1490 and trained the Paris scholar-printer, Josse Bade (Jodocus Badius). See S.H. Steinberg, *Five hundred years of printing*, Harmondsworth, 1966, 81-91.

38  Dunlop, *Acta*, 432 and 437.

39  Maitland Anderson, *Early Records*, 112, 114, 216. On Steinston and his book collection see Durkan & Ross, *Early Scottish libraries*, 145.

40  For Edward and Thomas Henryson, see *Oxford DNB*, Vol. 26, 597-598 and 601.

41  Durkan & Pringle, "St Andrews Additions", 16.

42  See the entry on Rolevinck by Katharina Colberg, in: *Verfasserlexikon der deutschen Literatur des Mittelalters*, ed. Kurt Ruh, Berlin, 1992, Vol. 8, cols. 153-158.

43  "John Lesley" (sic), in: *Oxford DNB*, Vol. 33, 417-421.

44  Dunlop, *Acta*, 204; Durkan & Ross, *Early Scottish libraries*, 110.

45  Eberhard Slenczka, "Die Weltchronik des Hartmann Schedel aus Nürnberg", in: *Quasi Centrum Europae*, ed. H. Maué, 284-303 (300-302).

46  I gratefully acknowledge the debt I owe, for their contribution to my teaching and research over many years, to former and present colleagues in the Special Collections Department of St Andrews University Library, and quite especially to Christine Gascoigne who, among much else, allowed me to use her as yet unpublished work on William Guild and his library.

# German Medical and Scientific Publishing, 1601-1800[1]

*William A. Kelly*

The juxtaposition in this paper of two seemingly unconnected disciplines is a reflection of a parting of the ways dating from the mid nineteenth century of two which had up until that time been intimately linked. Indeed it might still cause some surprise just how long this link lasted, when we consider that a prominent holder of the Keepership of Edinburgh's Royal Botanic Garden and the Chair of Botany in the University of Edinburgh for a long part of the nineteenth century, John Hutton Balfour, had trained initially as a surgeon, receiving his M.D. degree in 1831 for a thesis on the surgical treatment of gunshot wounds.[2]

A basic element of medicine up to the mid nineteenth century was botany, in that most medicaments were derived from plants. A true study of plants was both a result and a part of the intellectual movement which, arising in the sixth century B.C. in Asia Minor before spreading westwards to mainland Greece and southern Italy, culminated in Athens in the work of Aristotle and Epicurus.[3] Concomitant with this movement was the development of Greek philosophy, which led to a system of thought free from supernatural influences and an attention to the living world. In this regard Menestor can be considered as the first botanist, in that he studied plants exclusively, but it was Aristotle's pupil and later colleague, Theophrastus, who discussed plant morphology in his *De historia plantarum*, which made clear his deep interest in descriptive botany. The stagnation of botany after Theophrastus was part of the general decline in all branches of natural sciences, which continued into the Roman Empire and far beyond, the only real survivor being a discussion of medical herbs. This surviving interest was heavily dependent on the *Materia medica* of Dioscorides, the final harvest of Greek pharmacology, which was written around 60 A.D. It is an indication of the reputation of the *Materia medica* and of the restriction of the scientific interest in plants to medicaments down through the mediaeval period that Dioscorides' name was inextricably linked with botany, although the work's botanical content was minimal. That botany was thought of at all as a handmaiden of medicine was due to the elder Pliny's *Historia naturalis*. This was the only work apart from Dioscorides' list of medical plants to constitute through the mediaeval period and beyond a repository of plant, and specifically of pharmacology knowledge, which was kept in circulation by constant copying.

The dawning recognition of the rich variety of plants in the first half of the sixteenth century was quickened by voyages of exploration, particularly to the New World, of that and the preceding century. This quickening interest was shown by the founding of university chairs of botany, beginning with Padua in 1533, to which was attached the superintendence of the university's botanical garden.[4] However it must be admitted that this quickening interest had a deleterious consequence on the theoretical effect of Theophrastus' work, which was less than one would have expected because the botanists of the day were overwhelmed by the practical problems of having to relate these new plants to the descriptions of earlier botanists. Morgan makes an interesting connection between the obsessive urge of these botanists to describe with the same degree of attention each previously unknown plant and the insistence of the Reformers on the equality of all men in the scheme of salvation, no matter how low their background and social status might be. The validity of this connection can be seen in the adherence of many of these botanists to the reformed faith, who indeed in many cases, such as Rembert Dodoens (1517-1585), Charles de l'Ecluse (1525-1609) and Matthias de l'Obel (1538-1616), were obliged to move north to the Dutch Republic to escape persecution by the Roman Catholic Church.[5]

A considerable advance in botany was made by the advent of the herbarium at that time. Although the need for more realistic illustration of plants from living specimens was set back initially by the invention of printing, the necessary advances were met by two Germans, Otto Brunfels, who published his *Herbarum vivae icones* (Strassburg, 1530), and by Leonhard Fuchs, whose *De historia stirpium* appeared at Tübingen in 1542. Another German botanist and pharmacologist, Valerius Cordus, made it his task to give a detailed and systematic description of each plant in his notes on Dioscorides' *Materia medica*, which he added to his edition of his father, Euricius', *Botanologicon* (Paris, 1551).[6]

Many of the theories put forward, and their resultant discoveries, in botany and other unrelated branches of science in the seventeenth and eighteenth century were connected with the quickening spirit of enquiry which was designated in the latter century by the term, Enlightenment. An important and initially surprising development in these centuries which affected the much later course of botanical history was the number of Germans who began to report the results of groundbreaking research. The description of this development as initially surprising is valid, because it was achieved in spite of the generally small, backward states which made up the Holy Roman Empire at that time. However the more ambitious rulers of these small states wished to model their territory on Paris and so established in these centuries a number of new universities, most of which, despite a general lack of overall investment, had a medical faculty whose chairs included as standard one in botany. Another interesting development in science was that the political and social stagnation of the Holy Roman Empire turned the minds of the intelligentsia to philosophy, a trend which showed itself particularly in the nineteenth century.[7]

Among those Germans whose researches furthered botanical research either immediately or at a remove with others' help was Johann Rudolf

Camerer (1604-1668), whose discovery of the sexuality of plants had not been taken up by botanists generally, but had to rely on his compatriot, Johann Gottlieb Kölreuter (1733-1806), who was determined to prove Camerer's thesis beyond any doubt. This he achieved in his *Vorläufige Nachricht von einigen das Geschlecht der Pflanzen betreffenden Versuchen und Beobachtungen* (Leipzig, 1761) and his three volumes of *Fortsetzungen* (Leipzig, 1761 and 1766), in which, by using Camerer's simple techniques, he established his findings by his own logical planning and methodology.[8] Another German botanist of talent, and a fellow medical student of Kölreuter, was Josef Gärtner, who set himself the task of making a comparative study of all known fruits and their seeds, which resulted in his two-volume *De fructibus et seminibus plantarum* (Stuttgart, 1788-1791). Once more the history of botany showed the acceptance of Kölreuter's observations on the pollination of flowers by insects being achieved without much excitement being generated.[9] It was left to another German, a Lutheran pastor without any formal training in medicine or botany, Christian Conrad Sprengel, to examine and record the relationship between flowers and their pollinating insects in his four-volume *Das entdeckte Geheimniss der Natur im Bau und in der Befruchtung der Blumen* (Berlin, 1793).[10]

Science, if at a fairly general level, and at that strongly dependent on the teaching of Aristotle, was still taught as part of the normal curriculum in the Philosophical Faculty of German universities until late in the seventeenth century, as we know from the career of, among others, Hermann Conring, the Frisian-born polymath (something of a joke in itself, as those who know Germany well can appreciate), in whom I have a long-standing interest, was one of the intellectually brightest lights of an institution, the Academia Julia at Helmstedt, which was described with justification by one of its historians as the jewel in the crown of Germany's Protestant tertiary educational system.[11] This living continuation of the medieval system of tertiary education was designed to drill students in the basic elements of human knowledge before they embarked on the more intellectually rigorous, specialised subjects of medicine, law or theology. Several examples of this general coverage of science can be seen in the disputations presided over by the early seventeenth century Wittenberg academic, Jacob Martini [Ill. 1], and by a later one at Jena, Caspar Posner [Ill. 2-3]. Indeed a post involving the teaching of basic Aristotelian science as well as logic, metaphysics and rhetoric in a Philosophical Faculty was very often a necessary first step in the career of someone who hoped to secure a post later in one of the higher faculties, as we can see from the career of Johann Andreas Schmidt. The holder of a doctorate in theology, he had to spend several years teaching the above-mentioned subjects in the Philosophical Faculty at Jena before being recalled to the Faculty of Theology at his alma mater, Helmstedt, where he stayed until his death.

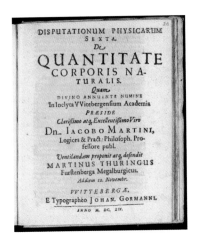

Ill. 1: Jacob Martini, *Disputationum physicarum sexta, de quantitate corporis naturalis.* Wittebergae, 1614.

Ill. 2: Caspar Posner, *De pluvia sanguine.* Jenae, 1670.

Important as this foundation-level grounding in science was in the general curriculum of the German, and other, universities of the time, we have ample evidence of the more advanced work done on various aspects of science there. A particularly good example can be found in the University of Altdorf, an institution which has never had the complete scholarly attention or, as my increasing acquaintance with its history convinces me the more, the credit it merits.[12] One of the most interesting members of its teaching staff was Johann Christoph Sturm (1635-1703), who, after attending the universities of Jena and Leyden and working for some years as a Lutheran clergyman, taught physics and mathematics at Altdorf from 1669 until his death.[13] He himself made no original contribution to the natural sciences, but he is important in the general history of systematic experimentation, whose role in producing and testing theories of natural philosophy was gradually accepted in the second half of the seventeenth century. At Altdorf he established a *Collegium experimentale*, at meetings of which he demonstrated a particular theory of mechanics or physics to a selected group of twenty, dubbed by him 'naturae scrutatores', who were invited to discuss the outcome of the experiment and its implications. These discussions were published in two volumes first between 1676 and 1685 and later between 1701, when he still alive, and 1715. Thus the wider scientific world was made aware of his mechanistic theory of nature. For Sturm experimental science was a part of a more general method of philosophical inquiry, which he called *philosophia eclectica* or *philosophia eclectiva*. The term, *eclectica* or *eclectiva*, was deliberately chosen to describe his attempt, as expanded in his *Physica eclectica* of 1697, to resolve by experiments on specific aspects of natural philosophy the disagreements among natural philosophers, who, he felt, were too hide-bound by their adherence to a particular school or sect, whether it be Aristotelian, Cartesian, Gassendist or Neo-Platonist, to accept that no one school had all the answers to the questions raised about the nature of the physical world. Eclectics such as Sturm regarded all philosophical beliefs to be provisional and open to modification. There are significant similarities between the stance taken by Sturm and Boyle, which can be seen in Sturm's defence of the latter's *Tractatus de ipsa natura* in the *Leipzig Acta eruditorum* in the course of a debate with Leibniz. Both of them showed a marked reluctance to engage in speculative arguments, which could not be upheld by experimental evidence. The insistence which each shared on the limited, provisional nature of philosophical theories was mirrored in their belief in the limits of human reason to draw universally true conclusions. This shared belief was theological in its basis. I do not know if Sturm was aware of Boyle's establishment of an annual theological lecture, which I believe still exists, but he would undoubtedly have approved of it. For them human reason was incapable of understanding divine nature and the reasons why God acted in a particular way. To come back to Leibniz, Sturm took issue with him in assuming that God acted according to rules

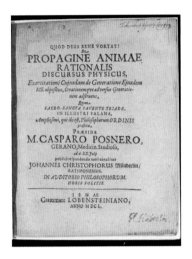

Ill. 3: Caspar Posner, *De propagine animae rationalis discurus physicus.* Ienae, 1650.

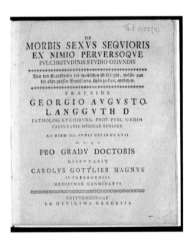

Ill. 4: Georg August Langguth, *De morbis sexus sequioris ex nimio perversoque pulchritudinis studio oriundis.* Wittenbergae, 1757.

set up by finite human reason. Sturm's experimental method shows us the importance of the relationship between the scientific and non-scientific debate which was active at the end of the seventeenth and the beginning of the eighteenth century. We can see the same disharmony between the mechanistic and organistic schools of medicine which was evident at the University of Halle between its two earliest professors, Friedrich Hoffmann and Georg Ernst Stahl. It has been argued that the disagreements between Leibniz and Newtonians such as Samuel Clarke were similarly as much about free will and religion as about natural philosophy.

No investigation of tertiary education or scholarly publishing in Germany in the hand press period can proceed very far without one encountering university dissertations. In saying that I am not giving vent to my own personal King Charles' head, for they unquestionably played an enormous part in the teaching role of these institutions. It is, however, a sad fact that they and their supra-bibliographical importance are still in the position of step-children, at best tolerated but largely unregarded. It is a sad fact that the absence of these from Willems' and Goldsmid's bibliography of the various branches of the Elzevier family has done little to lessen their perception as unfit for serious bibliographical research.[14] For that reason I was delighted to hear a doctoral candidate at the University of Amsterdam, to whom I was introduced earlier this year in the National Library of Scotland, assure me that she considers that her study of the Utrecht printer, François Halma, and by extension the record of Dutch printing during his years of activity, would be grossly incomplete without the inclusion of a bibliography of the numerous dissertations which came from his press. I can illustrate the fact from another of my long-standing interests in German bibliography, legal publications, that, although many dissertations, even up to doctoral level, served their immediate purpose of proving the candidate's ability to defend an argument in public before descending into intellectual and bibliographical obscurity. I have somewhat annoyingly sketchy, but, I do not doubt, reliable details on the database of one of my bibliographical projects of several doctoral dissertations, of which I cannot find a copy on any modern electronic database, including the very useful *Karlsruher Virtueller Katalog*. That said, the intellectual value of a good number of them can be shown from the fact that they were reprinted several, or even many, years after their original publication, indeed sometimes on more than one occasion. Such an example is that entitled, *Diaeta literatorum*, defended originally at Jena in 1674 with Georg Wolfgang Wedel as praeses, i.e. supervisor and often author, which went through at least eight reprintings, all of them interestingly described on the title page as 'editio'. Another illustration of the difficulty of compiling a bibliography of the dissertations defended within a specific faculty of a German university in the hand-press period is Werner Kundert's work on the legal dissertations defended at Helmstedt.[15] I was able to supply him with details of a good number of these texts from the holdings of the National Library of Scotland and that of the University of Edinburgh which he had not been able to find in any German library, let alone in that of the Herzog August Bibliothek in Wolfenbűttel, to which the holdings of Helmstedt University Library were moved after the closure of the university in 1810.

Despite the argument, which was put forward by some contemporary, influential academics, such as the afore-mentioned Conring, that dissertations were merely a rhetorical exercise to test the candidate's ability to conduct a public defence in Latin, and that the abandonment of the practice would not harm the educational effectiveness or scholarly reputation of an institution which took that course of action, there are numerous examples of medical dissertations, to restrict ourselves to one part of the topic which I have set myself, which tackled serious contemporary concerns, as the following examples will show [Ill. 4]. Georg Wolfgang Wedel, to whom I have also referred already, can be invoked again in support of the very practical nature of most medical dissertations by reference to the series presided over by him, which read, as they were meant to do, like extended case notes. The merest involvement with dissertations quickly reveals the amount of time and effort which many academics, including busy, highly respected ones such as Michael Alberti and Andreas Elias Büchner, who both made an enormous contribution to maintaining the reputation of Halle as an important centre of medical education which the founding members of the Faculty of Medicine, Friedrich Hoffmann and Georg Ernst Stahl had established.[16] The list, issued in 1740, of Alberti's publications runs to twenty closely printed pages, and my database, which still has much work to be done on it, contains details of two hundred and twenty of his dissertations, with almost the same number for Büchner. (And yet if we look at the map, which appears as both endpapers in *A history of medicine* (London: Nelson, 1945), by Douglas Guthrie, an Edinburgh-based laryngologist, whom the dust jacket mind-bogglingly credits with having devoted much time to a careful study of the history of medicine, we can only be grateful that Horst, Conring, Hoffmann, Stahl, Alberti, Bűchner and all the other German teachers of medicine were unconcerned about their future reputation in a far-away, offshore city whose intellectual importance can be easily exaggerated. I must confess that, after I had glanced at the contents of a copy of this item in a local second-hand bookseller, I was minded to put it back. However it was only after I had looked at the map that I realised this gave the work a distinctly absurd value [Ill. 5].) Having looked in detail at both the title and the text, often written in execrable Latin, of numerous dissertations offered for the degree of M.D. at the University of Edinburgh in the eighteenth and early nineteenth centuries, unsurprisingly I now question the bald, bold and frequent assertions of the value of that institution's degree.

The study of dissertations defended in an individual faculty can give us an excellent insight into the changing fortunes of that body throughout

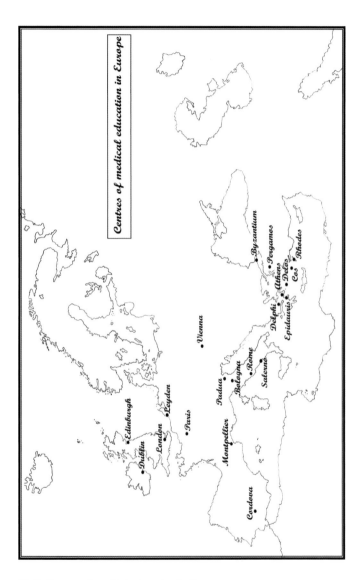

Ill. 5: Centres of medical education in Europe

its existence, whether it still exists, or does not, as in the case of Helmstedt
and Altdorf. If, moving from the particular to the general, we look at
those defended in one faculty of all the universities of a particular period,
we are able to see that different universities were a centre of excellence,
to use a modern phrase, at particular times. Let me illustrate this with
three individuals, the second and third ones having a common link in
the University of Tübingen. The first one is Lorenz Heister (1683-1758),
an anatomist, surgeon and botanist. Between 1702 and 1706 he studied
at Giessen, then moved to Amsterdam, where he pursued his studies
of anatomy under Fredrik Ruysch. In the summer of 1707 he gained
much valuable practical experience as an assistant physician in field
hospitals during the War of the Spanish Succession, following this up the
following year, after taking his doctorate, as a field surgeon at the battles
of Oudenarde and Malplaquet. In 1711 he was appointed Professor of
Anatomy and Surgery at Altdorf, a position which he exchanged in 1720
for a similar one at Helmstedt, where he spent the rest of his life. He is
credited with coining the term, tracheotomy, and was the first physician to
study the pathology of appendicitis. Not only by his lectures but also by
his publications he helped to improve the academic study and professional
standing of surgery. His most famous publication, *Chirurgie*, first published
in 1719, went through several German editions and was translated into
various European languages. Its popularity can be shown by the fact that it
was still in use as a standard text in the University of Vienna as late as 1838.
Of the second and third individuals the elder is Burchard David Mauchart
(1696-1751), who served his alma mater for most of his life as Professor
of Anatomy and Surgery. The mention of John Woolhouse in the work
mentioned here is more than simply one researcher acknowledging the
work of another, for Mauchart studied under Woolhouse at Paris between
1718 and 1720, interrupting his studies at Tübingen to do so. A pioneer
in the field of ophthalmology, Mauchart was the first to document the eye
disorder known as keratoconus. It is interesting that almost all Mauchart's
publications were in the form of dissertations. The younger is Johann
Friedrich Gmelin (1748-1804), who studied medicine at Tübingen, where
he graduated M.D. in 1769. He taught for a time there, before moving to
Göttingen in 1773, being promoted in 1778 to Ordinarius for chemistry,
mineralogy and botany. Gmelin's name lives on among chemists not only
in his published works and in the prize named after him which is awarded
by the Gesellschaft Deutscher Chemiker but among botanists in the name,
Gmelina, of an Australian-Asian tree genus and in the plant, *Artemisia
gmelinii*. Incidentally the early part of Gmelin's career illustrates another
common feature of German universities of the period under discussion,
that of the close family links which dominated their everyday life, for
Gmelin's father held a chair of botany and chemistry at Tübingen while
his son was studying there. The afore-mentioned Georg Wolfgang Wedel
is another good example of this phenomenon, having supervised the

doctoral dissertation not only of his elder son, Johann Adolf, who joined him on the staff of Jena's Faculty of Medicine, but also that of his younger son, Ernst Heinrich, whose academic career only went as far as supervising several dissertations before he became a practising physician.

Allied to the republication of numerous dissertations in monographic form was the practice of re-issuing them as part of a large, sometimes multi-volume, cumulation, a practice indulged in by some Dutch publishers as well as German. The evidence of their having been collected and edited by such highly respected figures as the Swiss polymath, Albrecht von Haller, who taught for many years at Göttingen, and the Dutch surgeon and anatomist, Edouard Sandifort, suggests that the initial impulse came from the editor. We know that both men, and part-icularly Haller, kept a close eye on new medical publications and Haller showed this interest in several important bibliographies which are still of great use today. This is of course not the place to dwell on the difficulty of accessing the contents of such cumulations; suffice it simply to say that a detailed note of the individuals involved, the title and the place and date of publication must be appended to the bare bibliographical details.

Closely linked to this particular type of academic publication, and one which deserves closer attention from bibliographers and intellectual historians, is the *Programma* or *Propempticon*. The earliest examples from the seventeenth century were simply an announcement by the supervisor or another member of the Faculty of the forthcoming defence of a dissertation within that body, with a short note of the candidate's family background and educational career, but, while it retained these last-mentioned features, it quickly developed into a format in days before the appearance of specialist periodicals for disseminating the author's most recent research, as the examples first by Johann Adolf Wedel, the elder son and colleague of the previously mentioned Georg Wolfgang Wedel, and then by two later members of the same Faculty, Georg Gustav Detharding and Johann Carl Gehler, will show. I should say at this point that I make no apology for drawing these examples from the same university, for my researches up to this point have proved to me that the medical and legal faculties at Jena disprove the general impression given by some histories of German universities in the eighteenth century that the whole town was an intellectual and cultural backwater. Part of the former assertion rests on the fact that very few of the professoriate was drawn in that century from outwith the local territory, but academic ability is always more important than place of birth. The fact that the early German Romantics found the town a more congenial spot than Berlin goes a long way to disproving the latter accusation.

We have comparable evidence from England of the rise in the eighteenth century in various German cities of non-professional societies devoted to scientific enquiry, of which the Naturforschende Gesellschaft in Danzig and the Academia Electoralis Moguntinae Scientiarum Utilium

Ill. 6: Jacob Theodor Klein, *Historiae piscium naturalis*, etc. 5v. Gedani, 1740-1749.

Ill. 7: Jacob Theodor Klein, *Summa dubiorum circa classes quadrupedum et amphibiorum*, etc. Lipsiae, 1743.

Ill. 8: . Jacob Christian Schäffer, *Die Egelschnecken in den Lebern der Schaafe*. Regensburg, 1762.

Ill. 9. Jacob Christian Schäffer, *Erläuterte Vorschläge zur Ausbesserung und Förderung der Naturwissenschaft.* Regensburg, 1763.

Ill. 10: Jacob Christian Schäffer, *Icones insectorum circa Ratisbonam indigenorum.* 3v. Regensburg, 1766-1769.

Ill. 11: Jacob Christian Schäffer, *ISämtliche Papierversuche. 7 Bde.* Regensburg, 1772.

Ill. 12: Thomas Arnold, *Merkwürdiger Fall der glücklich gehobenen Wasserscheu*, usw. Leipzig, 1794.

Ill. 13: Ignacio de Asso y del Rio, *Abhandlung von den Heuschrecken*, usw. Rostock, 1787.

at Erfurt are good representative examples.[17] If we focus on the former, we can highlight its significance by mentioning the work of three of its most prominent, contemporaneous members. Daniel Gralath (1708-1767) seems to have been particularly concerned with electricity, possibly his most enduring contribution being his bibliography of earlier published works, which appeared in volumes two and three of the society's *Versuche und Abhandlungen*, while Michael Christoph Hanow (1695-1773), who was appointed to the staff of the Akademisches Gymnasium in 1727 after completing his studies at Leipzig, published contributions on various aspects of physiology and meteorology. However the most prolific member of the society, who has never received the due he deserves from historians of science in Germany, was Jacob Theodor Klein (1685-1759) [Ill. 6-7], who produced several important monographs on fishes, birds and quadrupeds.[18] Important as these individuals were, by far the most prolific, most versatile scientific writer working in a private capacity was Jacob Christian Schäffer (1718-1790) [Ill. 8-11]. Educated at the Poeticum Collegium in Regensburg, he studied theology at the University of Halle from 1736 to 1738, before he became a teacher in his native town. In 1760 he was awarded the degree of D.phil. by the University of Wittenberg and that of D.theol. by Tübingen. In 1779 he was appointed pastor of the Lutheran congregation at Regensburg. A botanist, mycologist, entomologist and ornithologist, he published extensively on all of these. His scientific publications include his *Piscium Bavarico-Ratisbonensium pentas*, etc. of 1761, his *Fungorum qui in Bavaria et Palatinatu circa Ratisbonam nascuntur iconibus nativis coloribus expressae* appeared in four richly illustrated volumes between 1762 and 1764, followed in 1774 by *Elementa ornithologica*, in which he outlined a system of classification of birds based on the structure of their legs, in 1779 his three volume I*cones insectorum circa Ratisbonam indigenorum coloribus naturam referentibus expressae*, which included two hundred and eighty hand coloured plates of copper engravings of approximately three thousand insects and in 1789 his *Elementa entomologica*. As if this were not sufficient evidence of his versatility and energy, he also invented an electric pistol and a washing machine, conducted experiments with a variety of natural materials for paper-making and, to prove that he was more than a compulsive collector and taxonomist, he ventured to make proposals for ways of improving access to and understanding of natural history. That he was no local enthusiast, industrious but unnoticed and unregarded by the rest of the scientific world of his day, can be seen both from his membership of various scientific bodies in Germany and abroad and from his wide correspondence, which included the Swede, Carl von Linné, and the Frenchman, René Antoine Ferchault de Réaumur. He possessed a scientifically highly important collection of objects, which, rather than reserving for his own delight and that of other scientists, he allowed members of the public to inspect. One of these was Goethe when on his way to Italy. Lest anyone thinks that this industry was achieved as a result

Ill. 14: Henry Baker, Das zum Gebrauch leicht gemachte Microscopium, usw. Zürich, 1756.

Ill. 15: Francis Balfour, *Neues System über die … Intestinal-Fieber*, usw. Bresslau, 1792.

Ill. 16: Benjamin Bell, *Abhandlung von den Geschwüren*, usw. Leipzig, 1779

of neglecting his pastoral duties, he also published a number of devotional and pietistic works. It is no accident that almost all of the National Library of Scotland's holdings of his works, which, I have to say, are vastly superior to those of the library of the University of Edinburgh, come from the Dieterichs Collection, which was assembled by a contemporary senator of Regensburg.

We know from the rich secondary sources on German humanistic and technical literature of the eighteenth century that there was a great interest in foreign publications. An interesting example of such which combined a legitimate medical interest with a taste for the ghoulish is the *Glaub-würdige Nachricht von einer Dirne in Engelland* of 1735. However the majority of medical and scientific publications of this period, but especially of the latter half, were of a soberly professional nature. Some of these appeared in the original Latin but most often in a German translation. For some reason the publisher often issued them without the translator's name on the title page, but thanks to Bohatta/Holzmann and later investigators we know their names. It may be that the payment the translators received was considered sufficient remuneration for their work, but they were certainly no hacks, very often being medical practitioners [Ill. 12-16]. These translations also appeared soon after the publication of the original work, which suggests that some of the larger publishers maintained a group or groups of translators who could be relied on to turn out a translation in a relatively short time. The National Library of Scotland holds a good number of these translations, particularly of works by Scottish authors, as it has long been its policy to acquire these, but a particularly good repository of such translated works and other early medical and scientific imprints can be found in the Herzog August Bibliothek in Wolfenbüttel, with an appropriately excellent catalogue.[19]

Turning specifically to science, there is a world-class collection, which I am still investigating, on mathematics, physics and astronomy from German and other European presses, and also with an excellent catalogue, in this city. This was assembled by James Ludovic Lindsay, a member of a family of distinguished book collectors, who succeeded to the Earldom of Crawford in 1881. Having run his own observatory in Aberdeenshire for twenty years, he donated his astronomical equipment and his enormous library to the nation in 1888 on hearing that the modest observatory on Calton Hill was in danger of closing. His library, which numbers ca. eleven thousand books, contains the first edition of nearly every important publication in astronomy. For instance there is a copy of Erasmus Reinhold's *Tabulae Prutenicae* (Tübingen, 1551), on the motions of celestial bodies calculated on the basis of Nicolaus Copernicus' *De revolutionibus* (Nürnberg, 1543), which Lindsay also owned. Also to be found there are many works by Johann Kepler, including his most famous work, *Harmonices mundi* (Linz, 1619). However the star (no pun intended) of the collection, which reflects Lindsay's especial interest in astronomy, is the enormous number of pamphlets, more than one thousand two hundred, on comets. What makes this part of the collection particularly interesting is that in addition to rigorously scientific publications it contains copies of that very large body of literature below the strictly scientific level, i.e. popular reports and sermons, which allows us an insight into the commonly held beliefs on the significance of comets.

## Notes

1   A shorter version of this paper was given at the annual meeting of the Society for the History of Authorship, Reading and Publishing (SHARP), held at Oxford Brooks University from 24-28 June 2008.

2   *Oxford DNB.*, 3, 539-541.

3   In what follows I am indebted particularly to A.G. Morton, *History of botanical science: an account of the development of botany from ancient times to the present day.* (London: Academic Press, 1981). J.v. Sachs, *History of botany* (1530-1860). Authorised translation by H.E.F. Garnsey ... revised by I.B. Balfour. (Oxford: Clarendon Press, 1890) is still of value.

4   Ibid., 121.

5   Ibid., 125.

6   Ibid., 126. Cf. also A. Arber, *Herbals: their origin and evolution. A chapter in the history of botany 1470-1670.* 3rd. edition with an introduction and annotations by W.T. Stearn. (Cambridge: Cambridge University Press, 1986), 52-75.

7   Morton, loc. cit., 314-315.

8   Ibid., 316-317.

9   Ibid., 324-325.

10  Ibid., 326-327.

11  On Conring's medical and scientific studies cf. *Hermann Conring (1606-1681): Beiträge zu Leben und Werk.* Hrsg. von M. Stolleis. (Berlin: Duncker & Humblot, 1983); W.A. Kelly, *Hermann Conring (1606-1681): a study in versatility* (East Linton: Cat's Whiskers Press, 1993).

12  On Altdorf's place in the history of medical and scientific research in Germany cf. A. Cooper, *Inventing the indigenous: local knowledge and natural history in early modern Europe* (Cambridge: Cambridge University Press, 2007), 56-72. In addition to her useful, partial corrective on Altdorf Cooper is a mine of information on the subject outlined in her title. Further evidence of Altdorf's pioneering role in medical and scientific research is the establishment there in 1682 of a well equipped chemistry laboratory, the first such in the world, by Moritz Hoffmann, using university funds, cf. M. Ornstein, *The role of scientific societies in the seventeenth century* (Hamden: Archon Books, 1963), 231.

13  T. Ahnert, 'Nullius in verba: Autorität und Experiment in der Frühen Neuzeit. Das Beispiel Johann Christoph Sturms (1635-1703)', *Zeitsprünge*, 7/4 (2003), 604-618. An abstract of this in English can be found, entitled *The culture of experimentalism in the Holy Roman Empire*, which is available online at sammelpunkt.philo. at:8080/308/1/Ahnertdoc.doc

14  A.C.J. Willems, *Les Elzeviers: histoire et annales typographiques* (Bruxelles: Van Trigt, 1880). 2v. and E. M. Goldsmid, *A complete catalogue of all the publications of the Elsevier presses.* Edinburgh, 1885-1888. (Bibliotheca curiosa.) 3v. Goldsmid's claim (v.1, xxvi) to have examined every Elzevier imprint which he could find is negated by his confession that, as the former's bibliography is 'almost perfection', his is 'no more than a revised and abridged translation'. As an indication of the enormous number of dissertations published by the Elzeviers in the seventeenth end eighteenth centuries Goldsmid is as little use as Willems. For a corrective view of the bibliographical value of dissertations cf. S.v.d. Woude, 'De oude nederlandse dissertaties', *Bibliotheekleven*, 48, 1963, 1.

15  W. Kundert, *Katalog der Helmstedter juristischen Disputationen, Programme und Reden 1574-1810* (Wiesbaden: Harrassowitz, 1984.) (Repertorien zur Erforschung der frühen Neuzeit; 8.)

16  On Halle University generally cf. *Bedeutende Gelehrte der Universität zu Halle seit ihrer Gründung im Jahr 1694.* Hrsg. von H.H. Hartwich u. G. Berg (Opladen: Leske+Budrich, 1995). (Montagsvorträge zur Geschichte der Universität Halle; 2.). On Stahl cf. J. Geyer-Kordesch, *Pietismus, Medizin und Aufklärung in Preussen im 18. Jahrhundert: das Leben und Werk Georg Ernst Stahls* (Tübingen: Niemeyer, 2000). (Hallesche Beiträge zur europäischen Aufklärung: Schriftenreihe des Interdisziplinären Zentrums für die Erforschung der europäischen Aufklärung, Martin-Luther-Universität Halle-Wittenberg; 13.) and on Alberti cf. W. Kaiser u. A. Völker, *Michael Alberti (1682-1757)* (Halle, 1982).

17  Some information on the Naturforschende Gesellschaft at Danzig can be found in P. Letkemann, *Geschichte der Danziger Naturforschenden Gesellschaft* at http://www.staff.uni-marburg.de/~gornig/danzig/ geschichte.htm. The impulse to establish such societies in seventeenth and eighteenth century Germany outside the control of the universities and the part which they played in the history of scientific research there has still to be investigated. One such society, to which I have seen only passing references, is the Societas Ereunetica, which was founded at Rostock by the mathematician and philosopher, Joachim Jung, in 1622. Later he taught at Rostock and at Hamburg, where he continued to advocate experimental methods. On the Societas Ereunetica cf. M. Ornstein, op. cit. and on Jung G.E. Guhrauer, *Joachim Jungius und sein Zeitalter* (Stuttgart: Cotta, 1850), particularly 70f. Another

interesting individual whose role in the rise of scientific societies awaits research is Gottfried Erich Rosenthal (1745-1814), a baker in Nordhausen, who was a member of several scientific societies and the author of numerous scientific works, including the first lengthy bibliography of technology, *Litterature der Technologie*, usw. (Berlin: Nicolai, 1795). On the rise of scientific societies in early modern Germany cf. most recently S. Wollgast, *Oppositionelle Philosophie in Deutschland: Aufsätze zur deutschen Geistesgeschichte des 16. und 17. Jahrhunderts* (Berlin, 2005) generally and in particular 399-451 on the Societas Ereunetica.

18  On Hanow cf. *Allgemeine deutsche Biographie*, 10, 524-525 and on Klein cf. ibid, 16, 92-94.

19  *Verzeichnis medizinischer und naturwissenschaftlicher Drucke 1472-1830 in der Herzog-August-Bibliothek Wolfenbüttel* bearbeitet von Ursula Zachert unter Mitarbeit von Ursel Zeidler. (Millwood, N.Y: Kraus International Publishers, 1981-1987.) 14 Bde.

# Printing the Revolution: Berlin broadsides from 1848

*Susan Reed*

This is, as the title promises, a story of revolution. However, it is also a story of librarianship, and it is with that aspect that I must begin in order to define the main parameters of what follows, for it begins with a problem familiar to all librarians: a cataloguing backlog. In the autumn of 1998 a collection of hand-written nineteenth-century catalogue slips came to light in the British Library's German section, containing entries mostly of individual items in two large tract volumes of broadsides, posters and proclamations relating to the revolution of 1848 in Berlin.[1] These entries had never found their way into the Library's printed catalogue (BLC), which was officially closed in 1975. Indeed a note accompanying the collection specifically states that they are to be kept for reference only, although only a small proportion of them had in fact been printed and were thus in both the printed and online versions of the catalogue. We lacked the resources to (re-)catalogue the whole collection to modern standards, yet it seemed a waste of someone's long-ago labour either to dispose of the slips or to leave them as they were. Fortunately a team of staff, whose role was to amend and generally tidy up the online version of BLC, agreed to create new entries from a list based on the original slips. It fell to me to create this list, which involved going through the two volumes, checking the numeration of the items and the transcription of titles and headings on the slips, and, in some cases where there was no catalogue slip, actually creating some kind of entry which would accord as far as possible with the rules and style of the pre-1975 catalogue in order to fit in with those entries which already existed.

The two volumes of broadsides turned out to be a fascinating education in political and social history from primary sources. They include proclamations, reports, manifestos and satires, and are bound in chronological order, which gives a particularly vivid impression of events as they happened. Since the initial cataloguing project these and related collections, including a large volume of similar material from Vienna, have served as a basis for research and outreach to school, student and academic groups. They have also given me an interest in and knowledge of the subject which has fed into my activity as selector of German antiquarian material for the British Library. Although some examples from other sources both within and outside the BL will be used in what follows, my main focus is the two chronological volumes from Berlin, together with a third related volume containing mainly verse and pictorial satires,[2] and what they tell us both about the printing of broadsides during the revolution and about the events of the revolution itself. Of course this is not an exhaustive collection, nor is it a unique one. There are other collections in the UK, for example at the Germanic Studies Library in London University's Institute of Germanic and Romance Studies, and two major German collections, that of Frankfurt University Library and the Friedlaender Collection at the Zentral- und Landsesbibliothek Berlin, are available online in digital form.[3] Nonetheless the BL volumes under discussion form a large and significant enough collection to be taken as a representative sample of the kind of material produced and of the events which generated the greatest interest and comment.

The chronological arrangement of the sheets gives an idea of the scope of that activity, of the volume of material produced and the speed with which writers and printers reacted to events. In the two volumes 1851.c.5 and 1851.c.4 there are 662 items dated between 15 March and 30 November 1848.[4] For most of this period an unprecedented freedom of expression of political opinion was possible: press censorship was eased in mid-March but was reintroduced among other restrictions with the declaration of a state of emergency on 12 November. Many items in the collection carry a full printed date, in two cases using an idealistic formula such as '3. Tag des 7. Monates der Freiheit',[5] or can be accurately dated from their content, but even where this is not the case, all have been annotated by hand with at least the month in which they appeared. The month of June is best represented, with one hundred and twenty five items having either a clear date or a manuscript attribution to that month, and the storming of the Berlin Arsenal on the fourteenth of that month is one of the two single events which generated the largest number of items in the collection (the other being General Wrangel's entry into the city with his troops on 10 November). Even a printers' strike which lasted throughout August does not appear to have caused any significant reduction in the amount of material produced. Of course the collection is by no means exhaustive, but it is large enough to be taken as a representative sample of the kind of material produced and of the events which generated the greatest interest and comment.

Chronological order also demonstrates the speed of response to events. We see reports and reactions appearing on the same day as the events that inspired them. One item describes the same day's evening session of the Prussian National Assembly, and King Friedrich Wilhelm IV's appeal 'An meine lieben Berliner' was clearly rushed off the press as a response to the events of 18 March. Sundays and religious holidays – at least one item was apparently issued on Good Friday – were clearly no object to the printers, a fact not necessarily surprising where the latest news or an official proclamation was concerned, but perhaps more unexpected in the case of expressions of opinion or satires on recent events. However writers needed to get these into print quickly if they were to make any impact in what was essentially a news genre. To use a rather clichéd modern analogy, these sheets represent the Internet of their day: a forum for both official bodies and individuals to issue statements, publicise forthcoming meetings and rallies, report a day's events, and comment on the latest news or indeed on others' opinions of the news and events.

This analogy extends to the very public way in which much of this material was seen and read. Almost all the items in the collection are single sheets, printed on one side only and it is clear that the majority belonged to a culture vividly described by Robert Springer in a history of the Berlin revolution's street culture written shortly after the events:

> Denkst du daran, mein tapferer Berliner, wie wir des Morgens nach der Ecke gingen, um die neuesten Plakate zu lesen, das Heer der neuen Plakaten. Da hingen sie neben einander, das Heer der feindlichen Blätter; giftigen Parteihass athmete jede Zeile, jedes Wort; die eingesetzten Kommissionen hatten es sich wohl angelegen sein lassen, die ganze Tendenz, das ganze Gepräge der grossen Partei in wenigen Zeilen auszudrücken und doch hatte sie der indifferente Zettelträger in der blauen Blouse dicht neben-, oft übereinander geklebt.[6]

Many illustrations from the period show scenes of such busy street corners, and it is surely no coincidence that one of the most prolific of the printers represented in the BL collection is Ernst Litfaß, who in Germany gave his name to the street pillars on which posters are still displayed. Some sheets bear specific evidence that copies were intended for posting in this way: one, for example, warns that, 'Wer das Placat abreißt ist ein gemeiner Dieb'.[7] Street corner posters were a vital way of reaching those within society who lacked the time, money or level of literacy needed to subscribe to the regular press, and were important in raising the political awareness of this audience. Springer's opinion about the importance of this material is echoed by the modern historian Rüdiger Hachtmann, who states that, 'Nicht die Tagespresse sondern die öffentlichen Maueranschläge prägten das politische Denken und Handeln des "einfachen Volkes"'.[8]

The BL volumes offer a sense of this street corner culture as well as a history of the revolution in print; they also contribute to a history of the actual printing and distribution of this material, which I shall address before turning to the content of the material. The custom of adding the address of a printer (and sometimes a seller or distributor) to the imprint of placards makes it possible to create a map of the firms represented in the BL volumes, showing that most were based in the centre of the city and the grid of streets south of Unter den Linden. Springer names this as one of the most popular areas for selling broadsides, along with Unter den Linden itself and the Königsstadt to the east of the centre.[9] Some thirty nine firms are named in the BL volumes, but many are represented by only a few items, and some by only one. Most of the work was shared between a fairly small number of firms, and some of Berlin's larger printing houses are not represented at all, presumably because they concentrated on books and journals and had no interest in printing posters and other ephemera.[10]

Another piece of information often featured in the imprint of a placard is that it has been printed by 'Schnellpressendruck', i.e. using a modern steam press. Berlin printers had begun to adopt these presses from the 1820s onwards, with take-up increasing in the 1840s as the technology improved. Although there was some resistance to the steam-press among skilled hand-press workers, it does not seem to have become a major bone of contention and was not a real issue in the two Berlin printers' strikes of 1848 as it had been in similar Paris strikes in 1830.[11] Indeed the steam press came into its own during the revolution, being particularly suited to swift and large-scale production. Nonetheless it was by no means the main form of printing technology, especially among smaller firms; the prolific printer of broadsides Ferdinand Reichardt had two steam presses but a larger number of hand presses, while Eduard Krause, the printer of the liberal *Nationalzeitung,* only acquired his first steam press at the beginning of 1848.[12]

Krause exemplifies the liberal tendencies of many in the printing trade while also showing the differing degrees of radicalism among employers and employees. As one of the more literate groups of craftsmen, printers enjoyed a high level of political awareness and were often prepared to transform this into action. Krause trained as a typesetter, and was active for some years in a Berlin workers' association, the Handwerkverein. When he set up his own firm in 1845 this body initially provided him with much of his early work, and it was his politics, as well as his new steam press, that won him the job of printing the *Nationalzeitung.* He defended the barricades in March 1848, and would remain proud of this in later life, but as the owner of a press he later found himself out of sympathy with the aims of the August 1848 printers' strike, a position which lost him his work for the Handwerkverein.[13] Despite this loss Krause was on the winning side in the long run: the strikers failed to achieve their goals, and in any case enough stayed at work at least to keep up the flow of placards and broadsides.[14]

Another press owner, Ferdinand Reichardt, was even more of a convinced radical. As well as printing revolutionary material, he edited the radical periodical *Die Strassenzeitung,* and appears in the BL collection as author of a demand to know the truth about an alleged reactionary conspiracy in the Prussian *Landwehr.*[15] Springer offers a lively and admiring portrait of Reichardt but, although he depicts the printer as a somewhat Micawber-like character, forever short of money and forever coming up with new projects to make it, Reichardt must in fact have had a good head for business since he first set up as a printer in 1838 and, although his original firm was later sold, was still in the trade in 1864.[16] Printing, however, was not Reichardt's only career, and perhaps not his first one: Springer implies that he started off selling books, while at the same time running a sideshow in Leipzig. Another radical printer, Wilhelm Fähndrich, also came from a different background, having started out as a wine and tobacco merchant who, according to Springer, had at one time been incarcerated in an asylum for expressing liberal opinions.[17] This, and the fact that he actually acquired his press (from B. Schlesinger) during 1848 strongly suggests that he, even more than Reichardt, was in business out of conviction.

Of course some presses gained a name for printing more conservative material. Julius Sittenfeld was the most prolific of these, but Robert Springer, who describes him as 'gut, aber schwach', suggests that Sittenfeld became a printer of conservative broadsides simply because conservative writers were the first to bring him work and others followed as a result.[18] Given Springer's fierce prejudice against those he considered to be true reactionaries, we can probably take his assessment of Sittenfeld's apolitical stance at face value. Indeed press owners who held no strong political views, or who did not wish to combine politics with business, would have been chiefly concerned to keep the presses working. In fact the revolution could be seen as an excellent business opportunity due to the increased demand for printed material and printing was one of the few trades to prosper during the period. In addition the immediate nature of these publications and the fact that most were not intended for sale through the normal book trade placed printers in a powerful central position between authors and consumers. Of the thirty nine firms named in the BL volumes, eighteen were still in existence and run by the same individuals or families in 1864, while a further eight were under new management at the same addresses.[19] However, success as a printer of broadsides in 1848 was no guarantee of a firm's longevity. Reichardt's press, as we have seen, was still a going concern in 1864, as was Sittenfeld's but Fähndrich's business cannot be traced after 1851, further proof, perhaps, that he had acquired a press specifically to print for the revolution rather than as a long-term venture.[20]

Once the material was printed, it needed to reach its public as quickly as possible. We have already encountered descriptions of the street corner with its placards posted up, but this was not the only way in which this material reached its public. Broadsides were also sold from stalls in the streets, particularly around the centre of the city, but as well as static vendors, the period saw the appearance of mobile ones, the boys and youths who became popularly known as 'fliegende Buchhändler'. Springer describes them with an air of amused affection:

> Knaben der niederen Volksklasse, welche früher mit Kuchen, Blumen oder Schwefelhölzern gehandelt, vielleicht auch gebettelt hatten … umlagerten die Druckereien … um die frische Waare möglichst schleunig an den Mann bringen zu können … So kam der raffinierte Geist der Berliner Straßenjungen in nächste Berührung mit der Tagesliteratur und ihrem Vertriebe, und es war nicht uninteressant, die kleine Taugenichtse nun aus politischem und kaufmännischem Eifer die Leseübungen, zu denen sie sich in der Schule nicht hatten bequemen können, an ihre Waare,

bevor sie diese auf die originellste Weise absetzten, nachholen zu sehen.[21]

A doggerel poem from another source describes such a character advertising his wares, naming genuine satirical periodicals (including *Kladderadatsch* one of the few such journals to survive after 1848) and other contemporary talking-points:

'Manifest an unsre Wähler –
*Fliegende Blätter* und *Krakehler* –
Der Pabst hat sich 'ne Frau genommen –
*Kladderadatsch* – de Russen kommen –
Offne Brief an'n Boorgermeester –
Herzog Johann is Reichsverwester –
Menagerie blutdürst'ger Thiere –
*Freie Blätter*, nummer Viere –
Moneke ein Hochverräter –
*Neuer Berliner Struwwelpeter* –
Löwinsohn, Korn, Urban, Sigrist –
Birjerwehreken, sehst de, wie de bist –
Neues Extrablatt zur Voß'schen –
Die Cholera wüthet, vor eenen Jroschen –
Eenen Jroschen, man immer her!'
Das nennt man: Fliegender Buchhändleer.[22]

An interesting feature of this verse is that the references within it help to date it to early July: the Austrian Archduke Johann was appointed 'Reichsverweser' on 29 June, and Löwinsohn (or Lövinsohn), Korn, Urban and Siegrist (or Siegerist) were tried in early July for instigating the previous month's attack on the Berlin Arsenal, with sentences passed on 15 July.[23] The line 'Birjerwehreken, sehst de, wie de bist' may even refer to the title of printed satire dated ca. 7-8 July, although it is possible that both poem and satire were independently picking up a catchphrase popularised elsewhere.[24]

A more elevated image of items for sale comes from the masthead of a Viennese journal, the *Wiener Gassen-Zeitung*.[25] [Ill. 1] This shows an adult, rather than the cocky boy of the Berlin streets, distributing copies of the paper and a workman apparently reading one aloud to his companions. The scene may be idealised, but there is no reason to doubt that some broadsides, pamphlets or journals were bought specifically to be read aloud, not spontaneously on the street, but at formal or informal gatherings to those who either could not read or could not afford their own copies. Such self-referential descriptions and depictions of the ways in which they were posted, distributed and mediated are typical in broadsides and journals of the time. For example a piece conceived as an address from the 'Brunnen in der Breiten Strasse' to its provincial counterparts shows the fountain bearing a posted-up copy of 'An meine lieben Berliner'.[Ill. 2] However this is a double-edged image, referring also to an alleged incident where a piece

Ill. 1: *Wiener Gassen-Zeitung* (Wien: F. v. Schmid, 1848). Masthead of no. 9, 13.6.1848. (c) British Library Board. All Rights Reserved. PP.3437.cb.

Ill. 2: "Der Brunnen in der Breiten Strasse" – illustration from *Sendsch- reiben des Granaten-Brunnens an seine Collegen, die Brunnen in den Provinzen* (Berlin: Ernst Litfaß, 1848). (c) British Library Board. All Rights Reserved 1851.c.5.(23)

Ill. 3: *Constablers Leiden und Freuden geschildert in einem Briefe an seine Jelübte und veröffentlicht durch Aujust Buddelmeyer…* (c) British Library Board. All Rights Reserved 1851.c.5.(293)

of shell became lodged in a street fountain during street-fighting and a local wit posted the royal address beneath to emphasise the discrepancy between the King's peacemaking rhetoric and actual sanctioning of violence.[26] This is easy to overlook or misunderstand (even with reference to the text) and emphasises the difficulties for the modern reader in interpreting material of this kind, especially satires, as nothing dates more quickly than topical humour. However there are also refreshingly straightforward satires, such as one on the joys and woes of constabulary duty, which clearly describes and shows the narrator and his colleague, among other activities, arresting a young flying bookseller as he collects sheets from a stall to sell in the streets.[27] [Ill. 3]

This particular broadside, like *Bürjerwehreken, siehste wie De bist?*, is the work of Adalbert Salomon Cohnfeld, a doctor by profession and one of the most prolific satirists of the period, who usually wrote under the pseudonym of 'Aujust Buddelmeyer, Dages-Schriftsteller mit'n jroßen Bart'. *Bürjerwehreken* and *Constablers Leiden und Freuden* are unusual in Cohnfeld's output, in that they are not written in the persona of Buddelmeyer, who is usually the narrator and sometimes appears in the illustrations which generally head the sheets. He is often portrayed in a belted tunic, and always with his famous beard; his by-line became so well known that other satirists played on the name and description.[28] Forced to give up his daily broadsides in late 1848, Cohnfeld later edited a *Buddelmeyer-Zeitung* which ran from April 1849 to March 1853, and included more serious articles in standard German as well as the satires in Berlin dialect which had characterised his earlier output.[29]

The use of dialect by Cohnfeld and others causes problems of interpretation and was, even at the time, a double-edged device. On the one hand an author writing in dialect might be showing that he identifies with the common people, and is portraying plain-speaking, ordinary Berliners who are not taken in by empty rhetoric or political posturing. Alternatively the use of dialect could be considered as a deliberately mocking or patronising device, used by educated writers to poke fun at less literate citizens and portray them as ignorant and naïve. Certainly there were writers who used Jewish dialect as a device to perpetuate negative stereotypes of Berlin's Jews, although some Jewish writers themselves used the same device with benevolently humorous intent.[30] However, even where dialect was used with the best intentions as an attempt to communicate with ordinary people in their own everyday language, given that basic literacy is taught through the medium of the standard language, poorly-educated readers were probably confused more than anything else by these attempts to render their everyday speech. This was certainly Robert Springer's opinion; he describes the use of dialect as, 'ein Mittel, wodurch man sich irrtümlicher Weise verständlicher und eingäglicher zu machen glaubte' and makes the point that it is 'gesprochen jedem verständlich, aber gedruckt, dem Leser eine schwer zu entziffernde Aufgabe'.[31]

In fact, Springer's description of 'Strasseneckenkliteratur' and its reception emphasises the fact that, even without the added problems of dialect, some Berliners had difficulty in reading and interpreting any material they encountered, and often had to rely on the interpretations of more literate bystanders. But there may have been more subtle ways in which the less literate and even the illiterate could interpret what they saw posted up in the streets. Official proclamations, for example, generally follow a set pattern: the bold heading 'Bekanntmachung', one or two short paragraphs, and the name of the minister or body responsible. This format would presumably catch the eye of someone aware that such placards might carry important information about a new regulation which could affect their everyday behaviour. No doubt for this reason the same format was also used by groups and individuals wishing to contradict the official line and even to preach complete defiance.

Pictures were also, of course, a way both to appeal to the less literate and to help explain things to them, as in the example of the constable's story. However pictures do not always complement the words in such a straightforward way, and in a less visual culture than our own, political caricatures may have been harder for some contemporaries to recognise or interpret fully. Nonetheless visual clues which may seem obscure to us were no doubt more familiar to contemporaries. An example which we can follow today is the pigtailed bureaucrat, or rather his pigtail itself, which became a kind of visual shorthand for political reaction. [Fig. 4] Contemporary cartoons from a range of sources show such bureaucrats being trodden underfoot, physically held back by their 'Zopf', and even chased out of hell by the devil since 'selbst die Hölle haßt den Zopf'.[32] More purely verbal satires also take up the theme: in a parody of Goethe's 'Der König in Thule' the people cut off the King's long pigtail, only to see it preserved by parliament.[33]

fig. 4: *Tante Voss mit den Besen: Missionsblatt zur Bekehrung der politischen Heiden.* (Berlin: Löwenherz, 1848). Masthead of no. 1, 18.6.1848. (c) British Library Board. All Rights Reserved RB.23.b.188(1)

Meanwhile an anti-revolutionary piece turns the device against radical writers, describing a pamphleteer who terrifies the people by conjuring up ghosts which use their pigtails as cannons.[34]

A purely verbal reference which can also easily be traced through a range of broadsides, is the heading of Friedrich Wilhelm's appeal for calm on 18 March, 'An meine lieben Berliner'. We have already seen it being used both as a verbal and visual cue in the piece about the 'Granaten-Brunnen', but many other writers exploited it. Some directly copied the wording in order to criticise or subvert the King's message: a revolutionary placard headed 'An die lieben Berliner' (note the lack of paternalistic possessive) written not long after the original proclamation, warns against reactionaries, and in a satire headed 'An meine lieben Berliner!' the King announces his intention of bombarding the people of Berlin.[35] Other writers adapted the phrase, and some connected it with another satirical genre, addresses supposedly from the spirit of Frederick the Great. For example *An meinen lieben Fritz am 7 Juni 1848: eine Geisterstimme* in which the former monarch addresses his successor, or *Dieses Blatt gehört dem Könige: der alte Fritz an seine lieben Berliner*, which argues in favour of wearing the German tricolour (and also, of course, plays on the title of Bettina von Arnim's famous call for reform).[36] The phrase quickly became a cliché: one of Cohnfeld's Buddelmeyer broadsides is cast, perhaps rather wearily, as an appeal from 'die bekannten lieben Berliner'.[37]

For all the entertainment value of the satires we should not neglect the more serious items in the collection. Many writers expressed heartfelt opinions in as straightforward a manner as rhetoric would allow and were no doubt impatient with the satires, an attitude which can certainly be detected at times in Springer's analysis. Among the 'straight' political writers in the BL collection the best-represented is the radical demagogue, Wilhelm Held, who had been both a lieutenant in the Prussian army and an actor before turning to literature and pol-itics. He first published his journal *Die Locomotive*, in Leipzig in 1843; it was swiftly banned and Held spent the next five years in prison, emerging in the spring of 1848 to take up the journal again in Berlin, apparently at Reichardt's request, and to fling himself whole-heartedly into the revolutionary war of words. His broadsides are full of radical zeal combined with a strong belief in his own actions and opinions, which tended to come over as self-righteousness or self-importance and made him enemies on all sides. It also made him a target for parodists: to take only one example, an impassioned plea by Held on behalf of the starving was followed by a mischievous handbill announcing that Held himself, 'der Vater der Armen', would be distributing money to the poor.[38] Even Springer, whose analysis of Held is generally admiring, acknowledged the faults of the man he called 'Berlin's Mirabeau', and, writing only two years after the revolution, perceived that Held had already outlived his fame.[39]

Other serious concerns were reflected in the statements issued by political clubs. These might be invitations to meetings, attempts to drum up membership, or reports of resolutions and policies. Sometimes broadsides are issued in the name of the residents of a certain district, or of members' particular associations. These were not always what they seemed, and representatives of the groups in question sometimes responded in print to the original message, claiming that it did not in fact represent the opinion of all. To combat such accusations, some items, particularly petitions to government bodies, include a long list of signatories. Others state that such a list is obtainable from the printer, apparently giving weight to their claim to represent the opinion of 'Viele Berliner' or 'die pommerschen Bauern' but it would be interesting to know whether these promised lists really did exist; probably few citizens were concerned enough to find out and writers and printers, relying on this fact, may have made spurious claims of support for their work. News reports also made some appearances among street-corner publications, sometimes original reports, sometimes reprinted from the regular daily press, but on the whole placards and papers existed as parallel genres, even if the writers and printers were the same.

Most weighty of all were the official proclamations, generally printed by the firm of Rudolf Decker, official printers to the government. Decker apparently did not have a complete monopoly on official announcements, especially when there was something particularly urgent or important to communicate. There are copies of the proclamation, 'An meine lieben Berliner', signed by at least two other firms, Lessing and Jähns, and Ernst Litfaß also apparently printed 'die amtlichen Verlautbarungen, die zur Ruhe aufriefen und gegen die Demonstrationen wandten' in the early part of the period.[40] Other bodies with official or quasi-official status such as the Bürgerwehr and Magistrat used other firms to print their proclamations. Nonetheless the firm of Decker had borne the official title of 'Geheime Ober-Hofbuchdruckerei' for over sixty years in 1848, and its output during the revolution, as represented in the BL volumes, was almost exclusively of official material. These may be among the less exciting items in the collection, both visually and in terms of content, but they were central to the experience of the revolution and of course tell the official story against which we can measure many of the unofficial reactions.

Rudolf Decker also played an important part in development of the BL's German 1848 collections. A large number of the title-slips include the note, 'Presented by Mr Decker', with a number of different dates between September 1848 and April 1858, the largest number bearing the date March 1857. This is difficult to reconcile with the records in the Library's Corporate Archive, where there is only one reference to such a donation in February 1850. The material is described as a collection of twenty three 'ordinances, proclamations and other documents' in folio and quarto format, 'presented by Mr Decker, King's Printer, Berlin, through

Mr Asher'.[41] However Decker appears elsewhere in the records of the late 1840s and early 1850s as the donor of other material, usually the products of his own press and mostly presented via the Berlin bookseller, Adolph Asher, one of the Library's principal agents for foreign printed books at this period and for many decades beyond, or via other regular suppliers. It is possible that further donations of single-sheet ephemera came with these and were simply not listed, or were included under consignments of material purchased from abroad. Certainly there is a tantalising reference in the general Register of Printed Books (which includes both purchased and donated material) to '900 pamphlets on the Berlin Revolution' in a large consignment of purchased books from Asher. The designation, 'pamphlets', however, is problematic; it could be a catch-all term used to cover a collection of miscellaneous items including both pamphlets and broadsides, but it is unlikely that this is an error for broadsides, since further down the list the same hand records a 'collection of 162 placards on Revol. in Genoa'.[42] Clearly this, like the scope and origin of other 1848 collections, is another fruitful field for further research.

Meanwhile the matter of acquisitions brings me back full circle to librarianship, and I have two very positive last words to say from that angle. Firstly to my great delight a bid to conserve the collection was finally accepted in late 2007, and work began at the beginning of 2008. The large bound volumes were in very bad condition, with loose boards, torn paper mounts and damage particularly to the edges and corners of many of the larger sheets. At the time of writing the work is almost complete: the individual sheets have been placed in protective sleeves and are awaiting re-binding, making them more easily and safely accessible. Second, as a result of ongoing collaboration with the Department of History at University College London, whose students have been attending presentations on our 1848 Berlin holdings for some years now, there is now a postgraduate student interested in using the collection as part of the basis for his research into revolutionary satires. Thus I feel I can say, with I hope justifiable pride, that this collection has involved me in the central task of any librarian: to make accessible, conserve, exploit and encourage use of material in his or

her care.

## Notes

1   BL Shelfmarks 1851.c.4 and 1851.c.5.
2   BL Shelfmark 1851.c.6. This collection was fully catalogued, presumably at the time of acquisition.
3   1848 Flugschriften im Netz <http://edocs.ub.uni-frankfurt. de/1848/1848.htm>; Sammlung Friedlaender http:///www.zlb. de/aktivitaeten/digitalisierung/friedlaender. The Zentral- und Landesbibliothek website also hosts the online exhibition '4 x 1848:

Geschichten aus der Berliner Märzrevolution', http://www.zlb.de/projekte/1848/index.html, which offers a good introduction and overview.

4 Confusingly the numerical order of the shelfmarks does not match the chronological order of their contents; 1851.c.5 contains the earlier material and 1851.c.4 the later items.

5 1851.c.4.(67), Karbe's *Sendschreiben an seine Mitbürger*, 3.9.1848. This designation and a similar one from around the same time may be a reflection of ideological optimism related to the first General Congress of German Workers, which had taken place from 23 August to 3 September.

6 Robert Springer, *Berlin's Strassen, Kneipen und Clubs im Jahre 1848* (Berlin: Friedrich Gerhard, 1850), 134-135.

7 1851.c.4.(149). *An die Bürgerwehr*, September 1848.

8 Rüdiger Hachtmann, *Berlin 1848: eine Politik- und Gesellschaftsgeschichte der Revolution* (Berlin: Dietz, 1997), 44.

9 Springer, 143.

10 The main players are listed in Wilfried F. Schoeller, *Ernst Litfaß, der Reklamekönig* (Frankfurt am Main: Schöffling & Co., 2005), 65.

11 See Carl Koepfel, 'Die Entwicklung des Buchdruckes in Berlin während der letzten fünfzig Jahre' in *Beiträge zur Kulturgeschichte von Berlin: Festschrift zur Feier des fünfzigjährigen Bestehens der Korporation der Berliner Buchhändler* (Berlin: die Korporation, 1898), 280-303.

12 Springer, 139. – Kurt Wernicke, 'Als Unternehmer auf der Barrikade: Eduard Krause (1816-1882)' in *Bürgerliche Revolution und revolutionäre Linke: Beiträge eines wissenschaftlichen Kolloquiums anläßlich des 70. Geburtstages von Helmut Bock*, ed. Walter Schmidt, Gesellschaft-Geschichte-Gegenwart, Bd.21 (Berlin: trafo, 2000), 95-106 (98).

13 Ibid., 95-101.

14 According to August Potthast, *Geschichte der Buchdruckerkunst in Berlin im Umriß*, ed. Ernst Crous (Berlin: Verein Berliner Buchdruckerei-Besitzer, 1926), Anhang 1, XXVII, three hundred and thirty five out of around six hundred print workers in Berlin joined the strike on 1 August. Many of these returned to work on 15 August, after which the strike lost much of its momentum, although it officially continued until the end of the month.

15 1858.c.5.(146): *Offene Anfrage an die Commandeurs u. Wehrmänner der Landwehr*. Signed by Reichardt and Simon Jacoby. Shortly afterwards Reichardt printed a denial of any such conspiracy, provided by a Landwehr member in response to his first broadside (1851.c.5.(153): Brandt, Landwehrmann, *Erwiderung auf die 'offene Anfrage' wegen der Landwehr-Verschwörung*).

16 Potthast, 95.

17 Springer, 139.

18 Ibid.

19  'Uebersicht der Buchdruckereien Berlins und ihres Umfangs am Ende des Jahres 1864', Potthast, 93-107.

20  Ibid. - *Allgemeiner Wohnungsanzeiger für Berlin auf das Jahr ... enthaltend: die Wohnungsnachweisungen aller öffentlichen Institute und Privat-Unternehmungen, aller Hausbesitzer, Beamteten, Kaufleute, Künstler, Gewerbebetreibenden und einen eigenen Hausstand Führenden, in Alphabetischer Ordnung*, ed. J.W. Boicke, Berlin, 1823-1845, volumes for 1849-1852; available at <http://adressbuch.zlb.de/>

21  Springer, 142.

22  *Der Neue Berliner Struwwelpeter. Ein Politisches Bilderbuch fur reactionaire und Revolutionaire und solche, die es werden wollen. Nr. 1.* (Berlin: Verlag von A. Hofmann & Comp., [1848])

23  Rüdiger Hachtmann includes brief biographies of all four men in the appendix to his *Berlin 1848* (930-971). Löwinsohn was found not guilty and Urban given a short sentence, but Korn and Siegerist were each sentenced to seven years imprisonment.

24  Aujust Buddlemeyer, *Bürjerwehreken, siehste wie De bist? Eine Gardinen-Predigt, ihrem Gatten Ludewig beim Schlafengehen gehalten von Madame Bullrichen* (Berlin: Marquardt und Steinthal, [1848]). Reproduced at: http://edocs.ub.uni-frankfurt.de/volltexte/2006/5890/

25  *Wiener Gassen-Zeitung zur Belehrung des Volkes, geschrieben von Terzky.* Nr-1-130 (3.6.-26.10.1848) (Wien: Schmidbauer u. Holzwarth, 1848). This masthead illustration was used only on issues 8 and 9.

26  1851.c.5.(23): *Sendschreiben des Granaten-Brünnens in Berlin an seine Collegen, die Brünnen in den Provinzen.* See W.A. Coupe, 'The German cartoon and the Revolution of 1848', *Comparative studies in society and history*, 9, 2 (Jan 1967) 137-167 (153).

27  1851.c.5.(293): *Constablers Leiden und Freuden, geschildert in einem Briefe an seine Jelübte und veröffentlicht durch Aujust Buddelmeyer ...*

28  E.g. 1851.c.5.(318), 'Aujust Brandelmeier'. *Is Preussen det Volk? Is Charlottenburg det Volk? ... Ooch von eenen Dages-Schriftsteller, wenn ooch nich mit'n completten, doch mit ziemlichen Bart und ohne kahle Platte.*

29  Ursula Koch, *Der Teufel in Berlin: von der Märzrevolution zu Bismarcks Entlassung: illustrierte politische Witzblätter einer Metropole 1848-1849* (Köln: C.W. Leske, 1991), 121-125.

30  Horst Denkler, 'Flugblätter in "jüdischdeutschem" Dialekt aus dem revolutionären Berlin', *Jahrbuch des deutschen Instituts für Geschichte*, 6 (1977), 215-277. See also the linguistic analysis in Keith Spalding, 'The idiom of a revolution: Berlin, 1848' *Modern language review*, 44, 1 (Jan 1949).

31  Springer, 136.

32  *Fliegende Blätter*, Vienna, October 1848; reproduced in Herwig Knaus, Wilhelm Sinkovicz, *Wien 1848: Reportage einer Revolution* (Wien: Holzhausen, 1998), 261.

33  1851.c.6.(37). *Der König von Thule mitten langen Zopp: eene romantische Ritter-Ballade auses 11te Jahrhundert.*

34  1851.c.5.(239): *Vision eines Blinden.*

35  August Brass, *An die lieben Berliner* (Berlin, 1848); 1851.c.6.(6).

36  1851.c.6.(7); 1851.c.4.(3)

37  1851.c.4.(301): *Allerliebster Herr Jenral Druf! Man nich wider Kardätschen! Petition von den bekannten lieber Berliner, abjefasst und vorjedragen von Aujust Buddelmeyer.*

38  1851.c.5.(162): *Für die Armen!*

39  Springer, 126.

40  Schoeller, 65.

41  BL Corporate Archive, DH 53/2 (Department of Printed Books, Donations March 1848-January 1855). There is another reference in the same volume of the donations register to a gift of "German political broadsides and fugitive pieces" again in folio and quarto, and presented in late July or early August by a "Mr Zedner".

42  BL Corporate Archive DH 52/30 (Register of Printed Books, 1 January-7 November 1849). Nos. 648 and 710 of seven hundred and thirty three items purchased from Asher, 7 June 1849.

# Marketing Rules: changing publishing strategies in the Weimar period[1]

*Jasmin Lange*

In 1926 the publisher, Samuel Fischer, stated that 'the book is currently one of the most unnecessary things of everyday life'.[2] From his point of view the success of the new media, film and radio, as well as the interest for sports events and other leisure activities reflected the growing superficiality and profanization of intellectual life. According to him the public's renunciation of bourgeois traditions was one of the main reasons for the slump in sales on the book market, the so-called book crisis of the 1920s.[3] This paper explores how the book industry perceived moments of crisis from 1900 onwards. It will be argued that stagnation and depression were two of the main triggers for innovation in the book market of the period, facilitating new developments in book culture, especially in the areas of programming, book design and advertising.

The 'book crisis' was not just a phenomenon of the 1920s. Complaints about the market situation had already been a common feature of the book industry of the past decades.[4] Since the turn of the century the *Börsenblatt für den deutschen Buchhandel*, the main trade journal of the German book industry, published a vast amount of articles on economic problems. Experts came up with a long list of explanations why people did not buy enough books or why they did not read the right books. Overproduction, soaring book prices, new distribution channels, high payment requests by authors or simply the bad taste of the readership were held responsible for publishers' sorrows. Even the invention of the bicycle, and later the mass production of automobiles served as scapegoats for the publishing industry.[5] As the market expert, Bruno Conrad, stated in 1908: 'A publisher will always find a thousand reasons to explain a slump in sales. The only reasons he won't mention are his own shortsightedness, his lack of enterprising spirit and his disability to adjust strategies to current requirements of business.'[6] In the *Börsenblatt* Conrad asked his colleagues finally to give up on antiquated practices, to begin to establish a real relationship with the readership and to open up the world of books to the masses.[7] His interpretation of crisis is particularly interesting, given that he stated his opinion at a time when the book market enjoyed a relative stability. Sales figures were constantly rising and the target group was well-defined. Publishers were therefore complaining from a relatively comfortable position.[8] Nevertheless Conrad was right to point out that the conservative and over-regulated book industry in Germany needed a revolution in order to succeed in the future. He anticipated problems that became virulent only a few years later. After the end of World War

I publishers and booksellers were confronted with an altogether different social and economic context. They had to give up their 'splendid isolation' not just because this was a requirement for normal economic success but because this had become a conditio sine qua non of entrepreneurial survival.[9]

In his study, *Das Buch in der Krise*, the historian, Berthold Brohm, shows the different facets of the 'book crisis' between 1918 and 1933.[10] One of the main problems that booksellers and publishers had to deal with were the repercussions of post-war depression and inflation. The overall economic crisis had led to an impoverishment of the traditional clientèle of the book industry: the bourgeoisie could no longer afford to buy as many books as before the war. Workers and employees on the other hand experienced social and financial improvement of their living situation, which opened up a world of previously unknown luxury to them.[11] In order to guarantee the survival of the book trade, these masses of former non-readers needed to be convinced to spend their money on books rather than on cinema tickets or cigarettes. However publishing and bookselling strategies that fitted these new customers were yet to be developed. In October of 1921 the *Börsenblatt* author, Friedrich Wagner, pointed out this crucial factor: 'Well, everywhere we can see nice and modern salerooms with alluring books, but we haven't found an instrument yet to draw the non-reading classes to the book shops – even though it is claimed that these people's salary is higher than that of university professors!'[12]

This quote by Friedrich Wagner prompts a look back at the status of book advertising around 1900. As a consequence of the economic boom of the late-19th century most business branches were using a quite aggressive form of advertising. The entire urban landscape had become a canvas for economic communication. People received commercial mailings in the morning, were confronted with ads in newspapers and passed promotional posters on their way to work.[13]

German publishers and booksellers took part in this process of commercialisation only to a certain extent. In the milieu of the German book market aggressive communication and sales strategies were very unusual at that time. Publishers limited their activities to traditional advertising material such as standardised advertisements in the *Börsenblatt* or very basic brochures. Truly competitive consumer-oriented advertisement with eye-catching advertisements, mailings, flyers, posters and illuminated advertisement of brand companies, hardly existed.[14] Even more traditional than the advertising habits of publishers were the activities of booksellers. Usually they only made use of their shop facilities and poorly designed shop windows to promote their offers.[15] Anglo-American publishers had been talking about 'new methods of advertisement' from much earlier times, but these new methods were little discussed, let alone implemented, in the German book industry around 1900. Even the trade press described the advertising activities of German publishers and book sellers as modest and rather conservative. The marketing advisor, Carl Schöffer, wrote an article about this issue in 1921, entitled *Amerikanische Buchreklame* ('American book advertising'). He explained this reservation with the lofty idealism of the industry in his country: 'One branch of business after the other was captured by the American style of promotion, all of them participated, except for the German bookseller, who still holds on to his ideals (which by the way makes him superior to his colleagues from the rest of the world). [...] When using the word 'Buchhändler', bookseller, we still emphasise the first part of the phrase, 'book', while Americans emphasise the second part, 'seller'.'[15]

It would appear that Schöffer was the only expert who interpreted the practice in German book trade as a reflex of altruistic modesty. From the point of view of most contemporary book market and advertising experts, the book industry simply paid too little attention to the topic. The bookseller, Albin Watzulik, realized already in 1894 that there was an insufficient engagement and understanding of advertisement in the German book industry: 'The audience does not always want to see the same ordinary things, it wants to be convinced of buying a book by something new, something beyond the ordinary, hence something exotic and appealing.'[16] In addition to practical failures in advertising Watzulik and other experts argued that advertising lacked a sound theoretical basis.[17] Advertising theory in Germany was certainly inferior to developments in the USA. Still, books on advertising, not merely of the general kind but including specific branches of the industry, had been popular since the turn of the century.[18] None of these books, however, covered strategies for book advertising. The first designated publication, Alfred Metzners *Reklame im Buchhandel* ('Advertising in the book trade'), was published in 1909. This book filled the gap only provisionally. Metzner wrote at some length about the importance and the different types of book promotion, but he limited his very short study to the bookselling business.[19]

In addition to being a criticism of adverting practice and theory the early statements on book marketing by Watzulik, Metzner and others of a similar mind can be read as a commitment to modern commercial advertising. They regarded progressive, innovative advertising as an important precondition for successful sales and therefore as a necessary part of the cultural mission of the book industry.[20] In the course of the drastic post-war changes in society and the discussions about a 'book crisis' this attitude became increasingly popular. Moreover the discussion shifted from justifying the need for book advertising to proactive demands for improving the marketing methods of booksellers and publishers.

After World War I *Börsenblatt* authors published a vast amount of articles on professional advertising methods and regularly presented the newest research results to their readers.[21] In 1923 the Stuttgart based publisher, Poeschel, released the textbook, *Die Werbung fürs Buch* ('Advertisement for the book') by Horst Kliemann, a book designed to serve as reference for all future efforts.[22] Kliemann was a central figure in book publishing from the 1920s onwards. He had worked for several publishers, including Eugen Diederichs in Jena and Oldenbourg in Munich.[23] The success of his book was overwhelming, which he interpreted as a 'pleasing signal for the fast-growing interest and understanding of adverting issues in the book industry'.[24]

Besides such developments in the field of advertising textbooks, many more examples could be given in order to illustrate how book advertising became increasingly professional during the 1920s. One could point, for example, to the boom of professional seminars and advertising workshops or to the establishment of the first advertising departments in publishing houses such as Ullstein or Scherl. However one significant aspect will serve as case study: the development of cooperative advertising in the book industry.

In 1923 the Börsenverein der deutschen Buchhändler, the central organization in German book publishing, founded an advertising centre for its members, the so- called Werbestelle des deutschen Buchhandels. Already during the war observers writing in the *Börsenblatt* had initiated a debate about whether there should be some kind of coordinated, cooperative advertising. According to the requirements of war times some people wanted to centralise all cooperative advertising activities in order to save money and manpower.[25] However the Werbestelle did not start its official activities until October of that year. Although the project had taken almost seven years to materialise, the Werbestelle certainly was a great achievement of the book industry and even topped the efforts of other branches. No other branch of business had produced a similar centre for information exchange, procurement and general advice, a central office which acted as an 'advertisement think tank' for the book industry.[26]

In the wake of the changes in society the very agenda of the Werbestelle developed into something new. Before 1918 the future centre was supposed to rationalise advertising activities. After the war, however, advertising for reading in general became more and more important.[27] The new aim of the Werbestelle was to educate the masses and to convince them of buying books. One of the founders of the Werbestelle, Friedrich Reinecke, explained in 1929: 'Neither the Werbestelle, nor anybody else will be able to awaken those who are indifferent. A lot of people have also told me: Let them sleep, so there is more space for the ones who care! Sure, this is an acceptable statement, but it is of no use for the future of the medium book. We must realise that publishers are not just competing against each other. Publishers are competing against other branches of business. Therefore we must convince potential customers to value books more than smoking, going to the movies or attending other leisure activities.'[28]

Like Reineke a number of *Börsenblatt* authors justified the need for an advertising centre from a bourgeois point of view. According to their statements the masses needed to be educated, they needed to be told which books they should read and which they should buy. However Reinecke's declaration also makes clear that he regarded professional advertising as an important means to overcome the alleged book crisis. Experts believed that the Werbestelle should implement a generous and regularly recurring advertising campaign in order to strengthen the interest of workers and employees for the book in general.[29]

The Werbestelle met these demands with a plethora of activities. In order to improve book advertising in general and the activities of individual publishers and booksellers, the Werbestelle offered posters, master drawings, postcards with funny slogans, flyers and even promotional films. Moreover the Werbestelle organized shop window competitions, book festivals, reading events and public lectures about book publishing.[30]

The additional expertise became soon noticeable in advertising. Contemporary commentators realised that the design of advertising material had improved. Furthermore they praised innovative and target group-oriented publishing methods.[31] A look at the advertisements in the *Börsenblatt* illustrates these progressions perfectly. While in the 1910s they were of small format, of basic and almost standardised design, they changed dramatically after the war. Publishers presented their products with coloured, illustrated texts, trying to stand out by using concise slogans and texts. One of the innovators in ad design was the Berlin based publisher Ullstein. Starting from series of advertisements, to swatches pasted into these (for Ullstein sewing patterns) and real brand campaigns, Ullstein set the pattern for trade and consumer advertising in the 1920s.[32]

While the quality of advertising media improved, the quantity of advertising activities increased too. Curt Berger, the advertising expert at the academic publishing house of Johann Ambrosius Barth, noticed a huge rise in activities in the first half of the 1920s, which according to him had resulted in an 'advertising boom' in 1925.[33] His impression can be corroborated easily if one looks at the volume of the *Börsenblatt* from 1924 to 1926. The number of advertisements is strikingly higher than in the post-war years and the following years of the world economic crisis.

In addition to striving to achieve better quality and a higher quantity of advertising, new methods such as promotional films were discussed in the industry. In 1907 the *Börsenblatt* author, Bruno Senf, praised 'living photographs that are telling advertisement stories'.[34] Senf publicly supported the idea that book advertising should be modernised. In this context he pointed out that the book industry had missed an opportunity to make use of the new medium of film as an advertising means.

Senf made this observation at a time when movies were rarely used for commercial advertising. It is true that there had been attempts to show animated advertisements since the turn of the century, but the conditions for a professional use of advertising movies had been in place only since the 1910s. Among these conditions was the establishment of luxurious movie theatres for bourgeois audiences. As a consequence cinema as a platform for advertising began to interest brand companies such as Maggie, Dr. Oetker or Continental.[35]

In the autumn of the year 1911 the trade magazine, *Licht-Bild-Bühne*, reported the production of the first advertising movie for the book industry. This was a seven hundred and sixty feet long feature movie produced by an owner of an American newspaper.[36] In Germany, however, the proposal of Bruno Senf at first received only marginal attention. Advertising movies had their break-through only during the Great War, when politicians and the military discovered cinematography as an instrument of propaganda.[37] This development led to a stronger use of advertising movies in the commercial sector, so that contemporaries began to speak of a triumph of cinema advertising.[38]

At the beginning of 1920 the publisher, Walter Thielemann, wrote about the recent feature movie of an American library in the *Börsenblatt*. He encouraged German publishers to emulate this successful initiative.[39] In the same year Konrad Werther appealed to the readers of the *Deutsche Verlegerzeitung* that they should focus all their efforts on using movies for consumer advertising. Movies, Werther reasoned, possess an unlimited potential distribution and may stimulate the masses to buy books. Another important factor was that movie audiences paid more attention to films than to advertisements or posters. According to Werther there were three genres of films that were most adequate for book advertising: documentaries, features promoting individual products and cooperative features promoting books in general.[40]

One of the first documentaries of this kind was produced by the Leipzig-based fashion publisher, Otto Bayer, who issued family magazines and guidebooks for housekeeping. With his products he mainly targeted a female bourgeois audience.[41] In 1926 Bayer produced a documentary called *Lehrfilm der Kochkunst* ('Educational movie for the art of cooking'). According to journalists writing at the time the movie was applauded by everyone. Women flocked in throngs to specially arranged shows.[42] The Bayer movie not only enhanced cooking abilities, but the sales of the corresponding book as well. Driven by the slogan, 'Die Frauen wollen besser kochen lernen' ('Women want to learn how to cook better'), the publisher offered a special and cheap edition of one of his cooking books.[43] Motivated by the huge success of the cooking movie, Bayer established a documentary department that produced two more movies over the next two years. At last book market observers were convinced that film as a modern means of advertising should be among the marketing measures taken by publishers. As one of them concluded, 'if a company like the well-known fashion publishing house Otto Bayer in Leipzig has far-reaching connections and the best authors and graphic artists available for advertising, and still thinks it cannot do without film, this speaks for the value of film as an advertising means'.[44]

Documentaries served a double function. They provided information about the book industry and sent out clear advertising messages at the same time. In 1926 Friedrich Pollin published statistics in the *Börsenblatt* that showed five percent of all documentaries were about the book trade. There were more than forty films of this kind, propelling the book industry to seventh place in the ranking of most often dealt with industries.[45]

In conclusion, the increasing attention given to the topic of advertising resulted in a move towards professionalisation and modernisation of book advertising in the 1920s. Thereby the book industry tried to close the gap to other branches of business and the Anglo-American example. The influence of other branches or the USA is not enough, however, to explain these improvements. No doubt the reports on developments outside the German book market catalysed the interest of publishers and booksellers. However it was the economic, social and cultural changes after the Great War that forced the book industry to fulfil its potential of improving communication with customers. While the traditional book buyer experienced problems of liquidity, the new middle class, workers and employees were interested in modern leisure activities such as sports or going to the movies. In order to fight the rising 'book crisis', such was the conviction of book traders, this new middle class had to be conquered as potential book buyers. This could be achieved by targeting them with modern means of advertising which were modelled according to their interests. Within the span of a decade the formerly conservative and traditionalist German book industry had come to embrace book culture for the masses.

## Notes

1   The results presented in this study are derived from chapter five of my PhD dissertation, 'Der deutsche Buchhandel und der Siegeszug der Kinematographie 1895-1933. Reaktionen und strategische Konsequenzen' (Mainz University, 2008). For a fuller treatment cf. the dissertation.

2   Samuel Fischer, 'Bemerkungen zur Bücherkrise', *Almanach des S. Fischer-Verlages. Das 40. Jahr* (1926), 80-85(81).

3   Ibid.

4   Hans Altenhein, 'Die Krise im deutschen Buchhandel', in *Geschichtswissenschaft und Buchhandel in der Krisenspirale? Eine Inspektion des Feldes in historischer, internationaler und wirtschaftlicher Perspektive*, eds. Olaf Blaschke and Hagen Schulze (München, 2006), 71-81(71-75).

5   Jos. Thron, 'La crise du livre. Neue Beiträge zu ihrer Beurteilung von Jos. Thron', *Börsenblatt* 106 (09. 05.1904), 4061-4063(4061f.); Friedrich Schiller, 'Die Büchermode', *Börsenblatt* 141 (21.06.1906), 6128f; Ernst Waldmann, 'Zur Bücherkrisis in Frankreich', *Börsenblatt* 64 (17.03.1908), 3120-3123; Bruno Conrad, 'Bücherkrisis in

Amerika?', *Börsenblatt* 109 (12.05.1908), 5301f. and Paul Ernst, 'Der moderne Buchhandel', *Börsenblatt* 23 (29.01.1916), 101-103. On the sense of crisis in the American and British book trade between 1819 and 1939 see James J. Barnes, 'Depression and innovation in the British and American book trade, 1819-1939', in *Books and society in history. Papers of the Association of College and Research Libraries Rare Books and Manuscripts Preconference*, ed. Kenneth E. Carpenter (New York and London, 1983), 231-248(231).

6   Conrad, 'Bücherkrisis', 5301.

7   Ibid.

8   Reinhard Wittmann, *Geschichte des deutschen Buchhandels im Überblick.* 2. Ausg. (München, 1999), 295.

9   The editors of the *Börsenblatt* used this expression in 1914 to criticize the loose relationship of the book industry with all aspects of cultural and economic life. Cf. Anon., 'Dem neuen Jahr entgegen', *Börsenblatt* 1 (02.01.1914), 1-3.

10  Berthold Brohm, 'Das Buch in der Krise. Studien zur Buchhandelsgeschichte der Weimarer Republik', *Archiv für die Geschichte des Buchwesens 51* (1999), 189-332.

11  Current studies on the economic and social effects of the inflation prove this hypothesis only in parts. However contemporary representatives of the book industry and of other sectors of society were convinced of the impoverishment of the bourgeoisie. Cf. e.g. Anon., 'Propagandafragen', *Börsenblatt* 47 (24.02.1923), 230f.; Vorstand des Börsenvereins der Deutschen Buchhändler, 'Geschäftsbericht über das Vereinsjahr 1926/27', *Börsenblatt* 94 (23.04.1927), 449-462(450) or Werner Klinkhardt, 'Zukunftswege in die Buchhandels propaganda', *Börsenblatt* 69 (23.03.1926), 369-371(371).

12  Friedrich Wagner, 'Etwas über Verlagspropaganda und Verkaufsmöglichkeiten des Sortiments', *Börsenblatt* 231 (03.10.1921), 1453f. (1454).

13  Dirk Reinhardt, *Von der Reklame zum Marketing. Geschichte der Wirtschaftswerbung in Deutschland* (Berlin, 1993), 432-438.

14  Norbert Stricker, 'Buch und Reklame', *Börsenblatt* 283 (07.12.1918), 734-736(734); Hans Schmiedicke, 'Werbearbeit-Wertarbeit. Kritische Betrachtungen buchhändlerischer Werbemittel', *Börsenblatt* 72 (25.03. 1922), 379-382 and Wagner, 'Verlagspropaganda', 1453. On the standardisation of *Börsenblatt* ads see Annemarie Meiner, 'Die typographische Gestaltung des Börsenblatts seit 1834', *Börsenblatt* 28 (02.02.1933), 9-11.

15  Cf. e.g. Alfred Melzner, *Reklame im Buchhandel Beobachtungen und Anregungen* (Berlin 1909).

16  Carl Schöffer, 'Amerikanische Buchreklame', *Börsenblatt* 46 (24.02.1921), 225-227.

17  Albin Maria Watzulik, 'Buchhändlerische Reklame', *Börsenblatt* 144

(25.06.1894), 3854-3856.

18 Cf. e.g. Anon., 'Reklamekunst. Von Walter von Zur Westen', *Börsenblatt* 24 (30.01.1904), 995; Friedrich Schiller, 'Wiener Briefe XX', *Börsenblatt* 50 (01.03.1911), 2610-2612(2611) or Anon., 'Handbuch für Reklame für Kaufleute, Industrielle, Gewerbetreibende, Handlungsgehilfen und Reklamefachmänner. Von P. Friesenhahn', *Börsenblatt* 1 (02.01.1922), 11.

19 Cf. the detailed bibliography in Viktor Mataja, *Die Reklame. Eine Untersuchung über Ankündigungswesen und Werbetätigkeit im Geschäftsleben.* 4. Ausg. (München and Leipzig, 1926), 376-386.

20 Cf. Metzner, Reklame.

21 Cf. e.g. Friedrich Schiller, 'Fort mit der Reklame - es lebe die Reklame! Eine publizistische Erörterung in ihren Grundzügen wiedergegeben', *Börsenblatt* 140 (19.06.1908), 6758-6760; Metzner, Reklame, 4 or Viktor Mataja, 'Unterstützung der Reklameforschung', *Börsenblatt* 158 (10.07.1917), 806f.

22 The following selection illustrates the spectrum of articles published in *Börsenblatt* on the topic: R. Engel-Hardt, 'Buchkultur und Buchreklame', *Börsenblatt* 15 (20.02.1920), 57-59; G.A. Delbanco, 'Zur Psychologie der Reklame', *Börsenblatt* 67 (21.03.1921), 157-160; Hans Wehner, 'Der Tag des Buches', *Börsenblatt* 69 (22. 03.1922), 360f or Gerhard Menz: 'Zur Frage der gemeinschaftlichen Werbung', *Börsenblatt* 93 (22. 04.1926), 502f.

23 Horst Kliemann, *Die Werbung fürs Buch. System und Praxis der buchhändlerischen Reklame* (Stuttgart 1923).

24 Severin Corsten et al. (ed.), *Lexikon des gesamten Buchwesens.* 2. Ausg., Bd. 4 (Stuttgart, 1995), 238f

25 Horst Kliemann, *Die Werbung fürs Buch. Leitfaden der buchhändlerischen Reklame.* 2. Ausg. (Stuttgart, 1925).

26 Cf. e.g. Anon., 'Über die Errichtung eines Buchhandels- und Werbeamtes', *Börsenblatt* 180 (05.08.1916), 1039-1043; Jacques Jolowicz, 'Über die Errichtung eines Buchhandels- und Werbeamtes', *Börsenblatt* 200 (29.08.1916), 1125f. or Paul Nitschmann, 'Das Buchhandels- und Werbeamt', *Buchhändlergilde-Blatt* 11 (1917), 359-361.

27 Horst Kliemann, 'Von unserer Werbestelle und anderen Werbedingen', *Börsenblatt* 79 (02.04. 1924), 4495-4498(4495).

28 Erhard Wittek, 'Aufgaben und Ziele der Werbestelle', *Börsenblatt* 6 (08.01.1925), 267-269.

29 Friedrich Reinecke, 'Ziele und Aufgaben der Werbestelle des Börsenvereins', *Börsenblatt* 128 (02. 06.1924), 7800f.(7800).

30 Cf. e.g. Edmund Starkloff, 'Zur kooperativen Werbung', *Börsenblatt* 39 (16.02.1926), 210f.

31 Britta Scheidler, 'Werbung für das Buch' in *Der Börsenverein des Deutschen Buchhandels 1885-2000. Ein geschichtlicher Aufriss*, eds.

Stephan Füssel et al. (Frankfurt am Main, 2000), 226 – 233.

32  Gerhard Menz, 'Beiträge zu einer Theorie der Buchwerbung', *Börsenblatt* 19 (23.01.1926), 96-98; Erhard Wittek, *Das Buch als Werbemittel* (Leipzig, 1926); S. Heider, 'Ratschläge zur Werbearbeit des Verlegers', *Börsenblatt* 232 (04.10.1922), 1381-1383.

33  Cf. e.g. advertisment for the Ullstein magazine, Uhu in *Börsenblatt* 224 (23.09.1924), front page; advertisement for Ullstein-Bücher in *Börsenblatt* 173 (27.07.1923), 5725; cf. also Lavoby, 'Die Reklame des Großverlages', *Seidels Reklame* 17/18 (1921), 289-293.

34  Curt Berger, *Gedanken zur Buchwerbung* (Leipzig, 1930), 7.

35  Bruno Senf, 'Reklame', *Börsenblatt* 164 (17.07.1907), 7142.

36  Reinhardt, *Marketing*, 331-334.

37  Walter Panofsky, *Die Geburt des Films, ein Stück Kulturgeschichte. Versuch einer zeitgeschichtlichen Darstellung des Lichtspiels in seinen Anfangsjahren* (Würzburg, 1940), 75.

38  Hans Barkhausen, *Filmpropaganda im Ersten und Zweiten Weltkrieg* (Hildesheim, Zürich, New York, 1982).

39  Johann Friedrich Döring, 'Etwas von der kulturhistorischen Entwicklung des Werbefilms', *Seidels Reklame* 8 (1929), 377-381 and Arnulf Gnam, *Der Film in seiner Bedeutung als Werbemittel* (München, 1931).

40  Walter Thielemann, 'Die Einwirkung des Films auf die Leselust', *Börsenblatt* 11 (15.01.1920), 46f.

41  Konrad Werther, 'Der Film als Werbmittel', *Deutsche Verlegerzeitung* 21 (1920), 371-373.

42  Andreas Graf and Susanne Pellatz, 'Familien- und Unterhaltungszeitschriften', in *Geschichte des deutschen Buchhandels im 19. und 20. Jahrhundert. Das Kaiserreich 1871-1918. Teil 2*, ed. Georg Jäger (Frankfurt am Main, 2003), 409-522(507).

43  O. Moß, 'Der erste grosse Lehrfilm der Handarbeit 'Fleissige Hände'. Uraufführung Oktober 1931', *Buch- und Werbekunst* 9 (1931), 304-306.

44  Cf. advertisement of Otto Bayer for Bayers Kochkunst im Bild und Film in *Börsenblatt* 285 (08.12.1926), 12513.

45  Moß, 'Handarbeit', 305.

46  Fr.W. Pollin, 'Buchhandel im Film', *Börsenblatt* 190 (21.10.1926), 92.

# The German Paperback Tradition and Its Influence[1]

*Alistair McCleery*

## Introduction

The thesis of this essay is that a typographical tradition of paperback covers originated in Germany partly in reaction to the North American tradition that had infiltrated the nation through Groschenheft/ Schundliteratur. The US production of paperbacks, faced with competition from magazines for the same retail space in drugstores and markets, adopted the vivid colours and illustrations on the covers of these rivals to create a more flamboyant and exuberant tradition. This essay examines the twentieth-century development of the German tradition through Insel, Tauchnitz and Albatross to Penguin.

All of the defining characteristics of the twentieth-century paperback can be traced back to the nineteenth century and before: the binding and cover material, the convenient size, and the long print run. In Europe the development of the form had been closely linked to function. If books were to be rebound by their owners to create a more permanent and uniform library, then the publishers need only issue them in inexpensive covers. If books were regarded by their owners as relatively disposable upon reading, after whiling away the time on a railway journey or on holiday, for example, then the publishers need only issue them in inexpensive covers. If books were to be carried around a great deal, on a train or to the salon of a spa hotel, then publishers needed to produce them in conveniently portable sizes and weights. If publishers regarded their mission as the democratisation of knowledge through provision of good books at low prices, then they could reduce costs by reprinting, in long runs and in uniform formats, titles that had already proven themselves in the marketplace or critical cockpit. Such books, moreover, would sell through that pre-existing reputation (of title or author) rather than the visual appeal of the cover. Mass-market consumption did not demand self-advertisement of the individual title but it did require recognition of and confidence in the publisher as brand.

## Kulturverlage

A number of German publishing houses from the end of the nineteenth century promoted a German cultural nationalism through mass distribution of books regarded as culturally significant.[2] The 'Universal-Bibliothek' of Reclam, for example, comprised (and comprises) a large series of reprints of well-known authors at low prices that began with a liberalisation of German copyright law in 1867. The small format paperbacks (152 x 95.25mm), produced using stereotypes, were sold initially for twenty

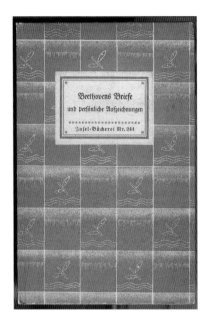

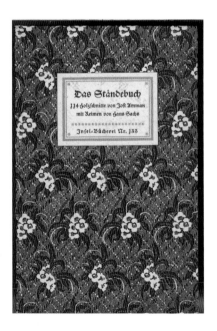

pfennigs in a standard Art Nouveau paper cover in red with a rose logo. In the 1920s the cover design became more self-consciously typographic, while the immediate post-Second World War volumes adopted calligraphic covers with the occasional line drawing. The more familiar undecorated, yellow covers were introduced in 1970. The standardisation of the Universal-Bibliothek lent itself in 1912 to the introduction of book-vending slot machines of which there were two thousand by 1917, chiefly at railway stations, mainline and branch, as Reclam exploited a hunger for self-education and a renewed cultural nationalism.

That same market was sought by 'Die Insel-Bücherei' founded in 1912 by Insel Verlag in Leipzig.[3] Insel, however, introduced higher production values, in design, typography and materials, to its books than Reclam. Consequently, its hardcover titles, though produced in print runs of ten to thirty thousand, sold initially at fifty pfennigs, more than double the price of rivals in the Universal-Bibliothek. That margin permitted the use of illustrations within the books. Boccaccio's *Decameron*, published in 1912, contained seven contemporary woodcuts while *Bilder des Todes* of 1917 was a vehicle for Holbein's illustrations, although it retained a typographical cover enhanced only by the use of rules. The standard Insel-Bücherei covers (until 1961) are decorative consisting of abstract or semi-figurative patterns (resembling wallpaper) with a label, stuck on or printed, that gives author, title and series data in the same Gothic typeface in which the text of all the books is printed. These patterns generally bear no relation to the nature of the title they distinguish: an edition of Beethoven's letters is covered in a faux-Japanese design of a twig falling into a stream and a row of grass or bamboo set in alternate squares while the woodcuts of Jost Amman are covered by a repeated flower design set against a tweed rug. What is important is that the cover pattern, no matter its precise nature, makes these volumes instantly identifiable as belonging to the Insel-Bücherei. However, the Insel books were not paperbacks. Only the exigencies of wartime restrictions in 1941 led to the adoption of paper covers; and the familiar board covers were reintroduced in 1951 by the West German Insel Verlag in Frankfurt (an East German Insel Verlag survived in Leipzig). Despite their low price the numbered volumes of the Insel-Bücherei were intended to be collected and retained by their owners; the attractive covers with their patterned papers promoted not the individual book but the brand.

Both Reclam and Insel anticipated a post-1918 yoking together of national moral decline and a crisis in the book trade. 'Cutthroat competition, overproduction of titles, high prices, the popularity of pulp and trashy literature, and economic hardships which led to the decline of libraries, research institutes, and readerships were the dominant elements in the chaotic picture of the German book trade market in the postwar period.'[4] The Kulturverlage produced good books at low prices. In doing this, they were addressing what was seen as the proletarianisation of

German society by co-opting working-class intellectuals into mainstream German culture. They also provided a visual contrast to the garish covers of the trash literature that was thought to be a major corrupting factor in the decline of traditional German values. Advertising the brand rather than the individual titles promoted confidence among both bourgeois and working-class readers alike. 'Reclam braucht keine Reklame.'

### Tauchnitz

Tauchnitz Editions in Leipzig was another such brand and, because it published in English, it became more influential in the development of the paperback and its design in the UK. Tauchnitz had established in the mid-nineteenth century a confident reputation for its reprints of British and American authors in an English-language paperback series not for sale in the UK for copyright reasons. From 1841 to 1937 it issued some five thousand titles, selling some sixty million copies in total, becoming 'the cherished companion of English-speaking travellers in central Europe and the royal road for foreign students to the treasures of English and American literature'.[5] All the great figures of English literature, particularly its Victorian novelists, were to be found in its easily recognisable but undistinguished format. Hans Schmoller remarked: 'Up to about 1930 there was nothing to commend the books typographically: they were squat volumes, rather too wide for the coat pocket, and set in small type with too many words per line to make for easy reading. The covers were white and almost identical with feeble title-pages.'[6] The fortunes of the company had begun to decline in the decade before 1930.

That Tauchnitz had not earlier collapsed altogether during the war itself and its immediate aftermath was due to the endeavours of its then Director, Curt Otto. However, its bare survival, without the necessary major restructuring in response to wartime conditions, specifically the closure of markets and lack of materials, particularly paper, left it in a weakened state to face the problems of hyperinflation that seized Germany until the introduction of the Reichsmark in 1924. The decision of the Society of Authors, initiated by John Galsworthy, to recommend to British writers (and agents) a change in contractual practice from concurrent UK and Tauchnitz publication to a delay of one year between former and latter compounded the problems of the publisher from 1926 onwards. Curt Otto died in July 1929 and achieved on his demise an apotheosis in the eyes of the Board of Directors. Tauchnitz Editions was reorganised, in that November, as a private limited company with all the shares held exclusively by the direct descendants of the first Baron Tauchnitz. Dr Hans Otto, brother of Curt, became the Chairman of the Board. Max Christian Wegner, formerly at Insel-Verlag, was appointed as 'Geschäftsführer', or manager-in-chief, with day-to-day responsibilities for the ailing firm but answering to a conservative Board very conscious of the company's traditions and glorious past. His appointment accounts for Schmoller's design 'watershed' of 1930 as Wegner set out to modernise Tauchnitz and place it upon a more secure footing.[7]

Herbert Kästner characterised the mission of Wegner's training ground, Insel, as the provision of quality books in volume at relatively low prices.[8] This goal emanated from the democratic ideals of its founder, Anton Kippenberg; Wegner was Kippenberg's nephew and shared those ideals. He wrote an afterword to Aurbacher's *Die Abenteuer von den sieben Schwaben* published by Insel in 1919; in 1924 he was one of a number of translators of the novels of Balzac's *La Comédie Humaine* issued by Insel in ten volumes; and in that same year he was responsible for the production of a catalogue of all Insel's titles since 1899. Wegner was a man of learning and cultural refinement; the high production values and aesthetic appeal of the Insel volumes reflected his own preferences. Wegner was 'Prokurist', or a company officer with statutory authority, at Insel before leaving to take over at Tauchnitz. He would have been acutely aware of the commercial need to integrate those production values with effective marketing of the brand. The decisions he began to implement at Tauchnitz from late 1929 until his departure in 1931 stemmed from that need, those preferences and those ideals.

Wegner introduced a coloured band to the Tauchnitz volumes to distinguish genres. 'A paper band, coloured to express the various types of works published, encircles each book; bearing a short description of the contents, it serves as an aid to booksellers and purchasers.'[9] He indicated the breadth of the Tauchnitz library by changing the half-title to 'Collection of British and American Authors'. However, it was not so much the design changes Wegner brought about as those he made to the company's publishing operation that led to his rupture with Tauchnitz. The odds were stacked against him: the nature of the literary market and of publishing practice, not least the delay initiated by the Society of Authors and the increasing role of literary agents, had changed since the company's heyday without the Board fully comprehending it. Where Wegner did attempt to rejuvenate the Tauchnitz list, he was frustrated by the Board. He set out to restore the financial health of Tauchnitz by cutting back on the size of the backlist kept in print. The general economic climate in 1929 militated against the tying up of company assets as stock in its warehouse. Wegner also took what would now appear to publishers the sensible step of divorcing the editorial and marketing aspects of Tauchnitz books from their production by employing two other Leipzig printers (and a third, when necessary, in Budapest) in order to secure the best price – eventually one of these, Brandstetter, was to predominate to the point of monopoly. No doubt, if he had continued at Tauchnitz, Wegner would have pursued further reforms including the modernisation of the cover design and typography. It was not to be – at least, for the time being. Wegner's surgery, however necessary, proved anathema to the Board and he was forced out of the company by mid-1931. Tauchnitz lost its dynamic Geschäftsführer.

## Albatross

Wegner's ideas, experience and drive were put to new use in the creation of the Albatross Press with John Holroyd Reece in Paris. The latter knew Stanley Morison, the noted typographer and designer, and also Hans Mardersteig, who played the major role in designing the modern paperback that Wegner had been frustrated in developing at Tauchnitz. Albatross Verlag was registered at the Leipzig 'Handelsregister' (register of businesses) on 26 November 1931, with Wegner named as 'Geschäftsführer'; he began signing contracts on behalf of Albatross that very month. The Board of Directors of Albatross included William and Ian Collins; its Chairman was Arnoldo Mondadori. Albatross was owned by the 'Publishing Holding Company', registered in Luxembourg and wholly owned by Sir Edmund Davis.

These cast members interacted to create the template of the modern European paperback and to base its typographical design on printing practice rather than illustration. The leading actor was Hans Mardersteig, himself a typographer and printer. Mardersteig had begun his career working for Kurt Wolff in Leipzig from 1917 but left for health reasons when the latter enterprise moved to Munich in 1919. Mardersteig set up his own hand press, the Officina Bodoni, at Montagnola di Lugano in Switzerland in 1922, where he produced three books for the Pegasus Press in 1927, 1928 and 1930 that were edited or co-authored by Stanley Morison. Mardersteig printed a limited edition in 1926 of an Italian translation, *Dell'arte della stampa*, of Charles Ricketts's 'A Defence of the Revival of Printing' (1899).

In 1926 Arnoldo Mondadori encouraged Mardersteig to enter an Italian national competition to produce the collected works of d'Annunzio; Mardersteig won and moved the Officina Bodoni to Verona within the Mondadori printing works. This was necessary to fulfil the conditions of the competition: not only was a limited hand-set and printed edition of two hundred and ninety copies of each of forty nine volumes on Imperial Japanese vellum to be produced but a further two thousand, five hundred copies of each volume were to be machine-printed on hand-made Fabriano paper. (The Italian state spared no expense for its national poet.) Through publication of these volumes from 1927 to 1936 Mardersteig demonstrated the successful marriage of high craftsmanship in typography and graphic design with modern production methods. Indeed, he was invited by Collins to Glasgow in 1934, at the suggestion of John Holroyd Reece, to inspect and provide recommendations for the improvement of the design and production of its titles. The Crime Club and Mystery Club titles published by Collins in the UK represented a key component of the Albatross list and Mardersteig was able to make direct, unfavourable comparisons with the typography and printing of other Albatross titles produced in Leipzig. (Early Albatross titles had been printed by Mondadori in Verona.) Mardersteig also had a hand in the production in the immediate post-Second World War period of the Biblioteca Moderna Mondadori of Italian reprints.

Much of Mardersteig's authority in undertaking this later work derived from his design for the Albatross Modern Continental Library in 1931. He chose for the Albatross books the more attractive (than Reclam or Tauchnitz) size of 181 x 112mm that matches the 'Golden Mean' of 1.61 and offers a good line length in terms both of reading and of the compactness of the book. The cover was typographical, adorned only by the black and white logo of the albatross with its long wings outstretched in an embodiment of the elegance of the whole design. The cover also contained the standard title, author and publisher details supplemented by the copyright notice - 'not to be introduced into the British Empire or the USA' - and surrounded by 'The Albatross Modern Continental Library: Paris: Hamburg: Milano', stressing its pan-European ambitions. 'To this day it forms perhaps, from the point of view of design, the pinnacle among paper-covered books.'[10]

Where Tauchnitz had introduced, under Wegner's management, a coloured band to indicate genre, Albatross, under Wegner's management, used the colour-coding of its covers: red for stories of adventure and crime; blue for love stories; green for stories of travel and foreign peoples; purple for biographies and historical novels; yellow for psychological novels and essays; and orange for tales and short stories, humorous and satirical works. (Silver was later used for volumes of special merit or length such as *The Albatross Book of Living Verse* issued in 1933.) The commercial success of Albatross books from 1932 onwards was in no small part due to the freshness and modernity of their appearance. Its visual restraint underlined the seriousness and quality of their contents. Both aspects, appearance and contents, placed Albatross ahead of its major commercial rival in the marketplace, Tauchnitz. Wyndham Lewis, for example, wrote to Stuart Gilbert in 1934 after he had visited Berlin: 'The Albatross editions I saw everywhere.'[11]

**Tauchnitz and Albatross**

From Wegner's departure in 1931 the condition of Tauchnitz had continued to decline, not least because of this competition from the energetic and youthful-seeming Albatross, until in mid-1934 it was put up for sale. Karl Pressler recounts, via Wolfgang Brockhaus of the august and eponymous German publishing house, the rumour circulating in Leipzig at that time that Tauchnitz was to be bought by a English publishing house, that is, Albatross, owned by a Jewish tycoon, that is, Sir Edmund Davis.[12] Pressler also paraphrases the question on many people's lips: was the old German company of Baron Tauchnitz to fall into the hands of a Jew, in only the second year of National Socialist government? From 1933 Nazi policy had been directed towards control of the media; publishing and the book trade were a priority for reorganisation. The Börsenverein lost its

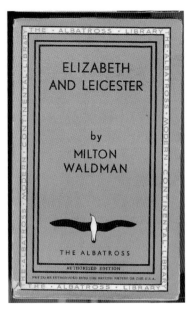

independence and purpose; the German book trade was controlled by the Reichsschrifttumskammer and its subsidiary, the Gruppe Buchhandel; and a process of Aryanisation was implemented in Jewish-owned or managed businesses. Whether the takeover by Brandstetter, the printing company producing by then most of the Tauchnitz titles, represented an attempt to avoid Jewish ownership or forestall Nazi intervention or both, it was clear that Tauchnitz needed a more assured editorial management than its new owners could provide. Wegner had maintained his links with Brandstetter, the company he had first brought in to print Tauchnitz and then also Albatross; he, in association with Holroyd Reece, had the range of contacts and experience necessary if the dying Tauchnitz were to be at all resuscitated.

On 1 September 1934 Max Christian Wegner resumed vicarious responsibility for the company he had attempted to save, if not for the intransigence of its then Board of Directors, four years previously. He did this through the agency of the Albatross, itself both a rival to Tauchnitz and a model of what a modernised firm could do. Albatross assumed editorial control of Tauchnitz while Brandstetter oversaw production. Wegner was now free to continue the process of modernisation he had been thwarted in previously. During the five years of stewardship by Albatross the number of Tauchnitz titles published mounted steadily, thirty-seven in 1934/35, thirty-nine in 1935/36, forty-two in 1936/37, forty-six in 1937/38, until 1938/39, when only twenty-nine were issued in a worsening German (and international) situation.

By 1936 other, more overt, positive benefits from the Albatross stewardship of Tauchnitz could be remarked: the original, rather squat format of the Tauchnitz editions, 164 x 118mm, was replaced by the more elegant Albatross; the books were made more comfortable to read by a change to Monotype fonts, Garamond, Baskerville, Poliphilus and Bembo; the shorter line length resulting from both new format and typeface facilitated legibility; and a coloured cover, derived also from the Albatross precedent and using the same coding, enabled easy identification by the reader in a rush. The paper band was abandoned. The short description of the book originally printed on the band now appeared in three languages, English, French and German, on the cover. The appearance of the two paperback series was harmonised, with resultant economies of scale in production, distribution and display, the only distinguishing device being the monogram 'T' for the Tauchnitz titles (designed by the eminent British engraver and typographer, Reynolds Stone, at Holroyd Reece's request) instead of Mardersteig's bird logo for the Albatross. The harmony and success were not to last: the Second World War changed Europe forever and the pre-War conditions could not be recreated. In particular, an aggressive UK paperback house, in the benign form of a penguin, enhanced by its successes during the war, began from the early 1950s to dominate the English-language market on the Continent.

## Penguin Books

Allen Lane in 1935 introduced this paperback imprint that was to overshadow all these predecessors, Penguin Books. The inspirations for this were both sociological, the quest for a new constituency of readers, and commercial, the successful precedent provided by Albatross since 1932. In September 1934 Allen Lane was a participant in a weekend conference on 'The New Reading Public' held at Ripon Hall, Oxford, attended by some fifty publishers and booksellers, and initiated by the then presidents of the Publishers' Association and the Associated Booksellers. The Conference was itself prompted by an article by Philip Unwin in the Bookseller. Unwin draws an analogy with the creation of a new newspaper-reading public at the end of the nineteenth century and asks where the equivalent of Northcliffe and his papers are in the book trade. 'Another new reading public has arisen, but the Book Trade has not yet been able to secure its support as did newspaper proprietors a generation ago.'[13] He highlights the growth of public libraries and in their use, the buoyancy of the market for non-fiction material made accessible to non-specialist readers, and the large audience for 'talks' on the BBC (radio). The potential of this market was not being exploited by publishers. Unwin argues that 'there is nothing wrong with either the quality or price of the product which the book trade offers to the wide public' and illustrates this with the examples of Everyman's Library and the Home University Library. (184) For Unwin the fault lay with booksellers who had not made their shops sufficiently attractive or indeed made much effort to attract 'the new reading public'. A general awareness of the existence of a reading public at the cheaper end of the market was articulated at the resulting conference, but few, if any, conclusions were drawn as to the best methods of reaching that market.

Hostility, based on the book trade's innate conservatism, welcomed the issue of the first Penguins. Harold Raymond crystallised the doubts and fears of the book trade related to Penguin in particular and cheap reprints in general.[14] The detractors of Penguins are characterised as 'open-minded critics who are anxiously wondering whether the book trade can afford to cut its profits to the fine point which a sixpenny novel nowadays involves.' (24)

> Many booksellers report that the sales of three-and-sixpenny, half-crown and florin reprints have shown a disastrous decrease during the last few years. Can the sale of Penguins at a gross profit of twopence a copy possibly replace that sale? The question also arises to what extent Penguins are finding an extra market ... In other words, is the converted public spending more or less on books as a result of Penguins? (24)

The real commercial inspiration for Lane's venture was to be found in the success of Albatross books. By the time the first Penguins appeared, the Albatross Modern Continental Library had reached volume two hundred and seventy two (Sinclair Lewis, *Elmer Gantry*). Allen Lane entered into discussions with John Holroyd Reece in 1934 about a collaboration between Albatross and the Bodley Head, of which Lane was then Managing Director.[15] These discussions included the setting up of what was to be called the 'Modern Library' in the UK on Albatross lines, co-publishing with Albatross which would continue to handle continental sales from sheets supplied by Lane. This is the system that was used for the issuing of Collins Crime and Mystery Club novels as Albatross paperbacks, although, in that case, the binding was also carried out in Glasgow. Albatross was also to advise Lane on the production details necessary to obtain the optimum economies of scale within such an operation. The key to the low prices of paperbacks lay not in the nature of the binding but in the cost reduction obtained through the economies of scale of a long print run across which fixed costs could be spread. From this proposed use of common printed sheets, as well as the concurrent Collins initiative, it is clear that the planned UK Modern Library would have adopted the same format as the Albatross Modern Continental Library and there is every reason to believe, given the part that the freshness of the cover design had played in the latter's success, that a similar typographical cover would have been adopted. In other words, this would have been a British Albatross with perhaps a different avian imprint and logo.

That the arrangement with Albatross did not come to commercial fruition was a result of difficulties in copyright licensing and of the precarious finances of the Bodley Head. The existing licences held by Albatross were, of course, solely for the continent of Europe; its books were not to be sold or circulated in the UK or USA as other publishers held the English-language rights there. It will be clear from discussion below that these publishers were very reluctant to cede any of those rights. Moreover, in 1934 the Bodley Head was in a poor financial state of health and in no state to enter into a collaborative agreement with Albatross. By the end of June of that year the firm was carrying a cumulative deficit on its Profit and Loss Account of £42,367.18.5; by the end of June 1935 a further loss for the year of £4,968.18.11 had to be added to that.

This is the context out of which the Albatross collaboration came to nought and his fellow-Directors refused Allen Lane the authority to go ahead, independently of Albatross, to create Penguin Books as an imprint of the Bodley Head, regarding it as a 'make-or-break' enterprise more likely to shatter the already fragile company. It is also the context out of which Allen Lane, his confidence buoyed by the Albatross precedent, went ahead anyway to found Penguin Books as a separate company, although the first eighty Penguin titles also carried The Bodley Head imprint on their covers – launched on his personal security and those of his two brothers. None of them was at that time wealthy and what they owned, they stood to lose if Penguin failed. It was, of course, an outstanding success.

Lane realised that marketing and distribution of the brand across a range of outlets were the keys to making Penguin a success. The tale of the origin of the penguin device has been repeated through most accounts of Penguin's history, although few acknowledge that this was in direct emulation of the Albatross's clean and balanced covers. Edward Young, the original artist, tells it in his reminiscence of the early days of the company: editorial discussions covering the entire bestiary had reached a stalemate when a secretary suggested a penguin; Young was dispatched to London Zoo to find this substitute for the albatross and 'the following morning produced, at first shot, the absurdly simple cover design which was soon to become such a familiar sight on the bookstalls'.[16] Of course the absurdly simple cover design owed much more to Mardersteig's original in 1931 with Young surely due credit only for the penguin icon replacing the previous albatross. When Beatrice Warde, the eminent typographer and educator, wrote that 'the typographic planning of these early Penguins was an exercise in discipline, good manners, and economic realism which would have reflected credit on the most mature designer', she was recognising the work of just such a 'mature designer', namely Hans Mardersteig.[17]

Lane wished to sell his brand of books to the reading public where it went, Woolworths and other chain stores, and in those places where it feared to enter, the bookshops. The key element was the brand rather than the individual title.

> In making what amounted to the first serious attempt at introducing 'branded goods' to the book trade, we realized the cumulative publicity value of, first, a consistent and easily recognizable cover design, and, secondly, a good trade-mark that would be easy to say and easy to remember.[18]

The cover and the logo were very successful. The company provided shops with huge quantities of brand-oriented display materials, centring on that logo and extending the characterisation of the penguins. In April 1936 Hudson's bookshop in Birmingham won a company-sponsored prize for the best window display of Penguin(s) while in May the whole of the front page of the *Bookseller* was given over to an advertisement for Penguin's 'Great Summer Sales Drive' and a sales promotion competition offering cash prizes to booksellers at seaside resorts and holiday towns for the most effective and original selling displays of Penguin books. Showcards were available in two colours; streamers in three colours; penguin cut-outs fifteen inches high; and long window strips, all advertising the brand, not specific titles. The standard typographical nature of the cover reflected and communicated the respectability and dependability of the brand. The use of an illustrated cover, as in the US tradition, would have vitiated that brand image being so carefully built by Lane.

### America and the postwar UK

However, the use of the word 'tradition' in this context misleads if it implies that paperback publishing itself had been of long standing in the USA. The illustrated cover was the chief selling aid of magazines, including the

pulps, that jostled for space and attention in the wide range of retail outlets *Publishers' Weekly* had identified for reprints. (Hardback reprint series in the USA such as the Modern Library, that introduced pictorial dustjackets in 1928, had always targeted a more sophisticated market and shown appropriate moderation in their design.) The first major US paperback house, Pocket Books, was founded in 1939 based on the Penguin model (eschewing the class of birds and choosing a kangaroo as its logo) after several ventures, including that of the Boni brothers, had failed in the preceding two decades. Its first ten titles were as conservative as those of Penguin four years earlier: a judicious mix of detective fiction, including Agatha Christie's *The Murder of Roger Ackroyd*, the classic, Shakespeare and Emily Bronte, the contemporary, Dorothy Parker and Thornton Wilder, and the title that defies categorisation, Felix Salten's *Bambi*. Nevertheless, in order to compete for readers, each title had its own distinctive cover, ranging from the semi-surrealist to the semi-photographic. Avon Books was founded in 1941; it was almost immediately sued by Pocket Books for plagiarism of format; Pocket Books lost – little wonder given its own debt to Penguin and the latter's to Albatross and Tauchnitz in this evolutionary chain of paperbacks. Avon's covers were even more striking than those of its rival; they ranged from the semi-photographic to the semi-pornographic. Title competed with title, lacking the emphasis on both brand and decorum characteristic of the European tradition.

In the UK itself, new competitors arose after the War less in thrall to the typographic tradition. In particular, Pan Books, founded in 1944 and issuing its first mass-market paperbacks in 1947, seemed to represent a less staid, more 'American' approach to cover design with its use of full-colour illustrations. The most significant titles on its list from the 1950s onwards, Ian Fleming's series of James Bond books, relied on dramatic covers both to reflect the 'snobbery with violence' of the contents and to reinforce its popularity to readers. Corgi, founded in 1951, followed suit in emulating American rather than European models. UK readers, increasingly surrounded by vivid advertising illustration, were also becoming more attuned to the visual.

The response of Penguin was to consolidate rather than change. Jan Tschichold was appointed in 1947 to take charge of typography and production at Penguin, a role similar to that performed by Mardersteig for Collins in 1934. This move represented a perpetuation of the typographic cover. Tschichold had started his career in Leipzig working for Insel on covers and binding and for Poeschel and Trepte, printers of Insel books, on typography and print production. His hostility to the Nazis led to his departure in 1933 for Basle in Switzerland, which remained his base thereafter. In other words, he was steeped in the European tradition of typographic covers and the reforms he introduced were chiefly to the standards expected from the many printers who serviced Penguin. He did tinker with the cover's horizontal colour bars in a manner that allowed for the occasional discreet line drawing or engraving. The continuity of the brand image, and the concomitant values of sensibleness and quality, was retained. This stemmed partly from the personal taste of Allen Lane, who despised the flashiness of American 'breastsellers' and partly from the fear of altering a successful formula.

Hans Schmoller, Tschichold's successor in 1949, when the latter returned to Switzerland, appeared cut from the same cloth, having also served his time in the German printing and book trade. However, during his long period at Penguin – he retired in 1976 – he oversaw change, at first gradual, then accelerated as Allen Lane lost his grip on the company, towards the use of illustrations for covers. He developed Tschichold's concept of a vertical grid to replace the horizontal that had been used since 1935 and, in this way, opened up the covers to further decorous illustration. The designer, Germano Facetti, began from 1961 to build on the traditional Penguin colour-coded series such as Penguin Crime to introduce elements of collage, illustration and photography in keeping with the nature of the brand and the individual title. The impact of these new covers was such that Facetti began to transform other series such as the Penguin Classics. The Penguin Specials, relatively dormant since the Second World War, were revamped to handle the issues of the 1960s, such as education, drugs and the trade unions; this overhaul included the revision of the traditional red covers to make each title more striking and more contemporary. The development of graphic design education within UK art colleges resulted in the ability to find and hire innovative designers capable of divorcing cover illustration and design from typography and page layout. The tendency to use visual covers must also be seen as a response to the increasingly visual culture of the time. Alan Aldridge was appointed as Art Director of Penguin in 1965. Aldridge paid little attention to continuity of brand image, treating each cover as a poster advertising that particular title. The result was a sudden flowering of colour and of witty and dramatic covers on Penguin books that owed little or nothing to the hitherto predominant European typographic tradition.

## Conclusion

It might seem a long way from Germany before the First World War to the UK in the 1960s, but there are two types of continuity. The first is in the perpetuation of the typographic cover by a series of designers through Mardersteig to Tschichold and Schmoller trained in Germany. The second lies in the continuing principle of the democratisation of knowledge through the publication of good books with high production values at low prices. The values of the kulturverlage were reflected in the public service ethos of Penguin, strikingly apparent in its history before and after the Second World War. Penguin Books, 'imbued with the ideal that everyman should be able to make an enlightened rational decision, strove to disseminate knowledge and ideas to a wider public.'[19] In doing so, it stood in both the design and intellectual traditions of Reclam, Insel, Albatross and other German publishing houses.

## Notes

1   An earlier version of this essay was given as a lecture at the British Library in June 2007. It also draws on some material first published in Alistair McCleery, 'The Paperback Evolution' in N Matthew and N Moody eds. *Judging a book by its cover* (Aldershot, Hants: Ashgate, 2007), 3-18.
2   For a discussion of the growth of neoconservative publishing houses acting as 'cultural publishers', see Gary D. Stark, *Entrepreneurs of ideology: neoconservative publishers in Germany 1880-1933* (Chapel Hill: University of North Carolina Press, 1981).
3   See Heinz Sarkowski, *Der Insel-Verlag: Eine Bibliographie 1899-1969* (Frankfurt am Main: Insel, 1970).
4   Gideon Reuveni, *Reading Germany: literature and consumer culture in Germany before 1933* (New York: Berghahn Books, 2006), 19.
5   S.H. Steinberg, *Five hundred years of printing* (Harmondsworth: Penguin, 1955), 354.
6   Hans Schmoller, 'Reprints: Aldine and After', *Penrose Annual* 47 (1953), 37.
7   See Alistair McCleery, 'Albatross and Tauchnitz: a community of interest', *The Library* 7th series, vol 7, no 3 (Sept. 2006), 297-316.
8   Herbert Kästner, *75 Jahre Insel-Bücherei 1912-1987: Eine Bibliographie* (Leipzig: Insel, 1987).
9   *Tauchnitz* Edition 1931 (Hamburg: Tauchnitz, 1932), 13.
10  Schmoller 1953, 38
11  Wyndham Lewis to Stuart Gilbert, 19 June 1934, Stuart Gilbert Papers 2.3, Harry Ransom Humanities Research Center, University of Texas, Austin.
12  Karl H. Pressler, 'Tauchnitz und Albatross: Zur Geschichte des Taschenbuchs', *Börsenblatt für den Deutschen Buchhandel* 8 (29 January 1985), A5.
13  Philip S. Unwin, 'A New Reading Public?', *Bookseller*, April 5, 1934, 184.
14  Harold Raymond, *Publishing and bookselling: a survey of post-war developments and present-day problems* (London: Dent, 1938), 23.
15  Confidential memo dated 1934, The Bodley Head Papers, University of Reading Library [uncatalogued]. See Alistair McCleery, 'The Return of the Publisher to Book History: the case of Allen Lane', *Book History* 5 (2002), 161-185.
16  Edward Young, 'The Early Days of Penguins', *The Book Collector*, Vol.1, No.4 (Winter, 1952), 210.

17  Quoted in Lynton Lamb, 'Penguin Books – style and mass production', *Penrose Annual* 46 (1952), 40.

18  Allen Lane, 'Penguins and Pelicans', *The Penrose Annual* 40 (1938), 42.

19  Nicholas Joicey, 'A Paperback Guide to Progress: Penguin Books 1935 -c.1951', *Twentieth Century British History*, Vol.4, No. 1 (1993), 56.

# Notes on Contributors

**Jeffrey Ashcroft** studied at the universities of Göttingen and Cambridge and has taught at the universities of Tübingen, Aberystwyth and St Andrews, where he is now Honorary Research Fellow in the Reformation Studies Institute and the School of Modern Languages. He has published on the history and literature of the Crusades, the Medieval German and Latin lyric, Bible translation before and during the Reformation, and on early printed books. Currently he holds a Leverhulme Trust Emeritus Research Fellowship for his forthcoming documentary biography of Albrecht Dürer.

**Mary Fischer** is currently Reader and Subject Group Leader for Languages at Edinburgh Napier University. She has published extensively on the literature of the Teutonic Order and the crusades. She is currently completing a major translation of Nicolaus von Jeroschin's *Chronicle of Prussia*, before moving on to a new project investigating publishing links between German and Scotland in the 19th and 20th century.

**John L. Flood** is Emeritus Professor of German in the University of London and a Past President of the Bibliographical Society (London). He has published extensively on the history of the book in Germany. His publications include *Die Historie von Herzog Ernst. Die Frankfurter Prosafassung des 16. Jahrhunderts* (Berlin, 1991), *The German Book 1450-1750*, edited with W. A. Kelly (London, 1995), *Johannes Sinapius (1505-1560). Hellenist and Physician in Germany and Italy* (Geneva, 1997) (with D. J. Shaw), and the four-volume handbook P*oets Laureate in the Holy Roman Empire* (Berlin and New York, 2006).

**William A. Kelly** was formerly an Assistant Keeper in charge of the National Library of Scotland's printed German and Low Countries collections. In his retirement (whatever that is) he is now an Honorary Research Fellow in the Scottish Centre for the Book at Edinburgh Napier University.

**Henrike Lähnemann** is Professor of German Studies at Newcastle University. She is working in the field of medieval German literature with a special interest in text transmission, image-text-relationship and digital editing. Her current project focuses on the late medieval devotional texts and songs from the Northern German convent of Medingen and Northern German mystical traditions.

**Jasmin Lange** received her PhD in Book and Media Studies from Johannes Gutenberg University Mainz, Germany, in 2009. Der deutsche Buchhandel und der Siegeszug der Kinematographie 1895 - 1933 ('The German Book Trade and the Emergence of Film 1895 - 1933') is to be published by Harrassowitz in the series Mainzer Studien zur Buchwissenschaft (forthcoming 2010). She lives and works in Edinburgh, Scotland.

**Alistair McCleery** is Professor of Literature and Culture and Director of the Scottish Centre for the Book at Edinburgh Napier University, Edinburgh. He has published widely on Scottish and Irish literature, particularly on Neil Gunn and James Joyce. He is co-author of *An Introduction to Book History* (2005) and *The Book History Reader* (second edition, 2006). He was co-editor of the *History of the Book in Scotland 1880-1980* published by Edinburgh University Press in 2007.

**Susan Reed** is Head of German Collections at the British Library. As well as the Revolution of 1848 her research interests include the German book-trade in nineteenth-century Britain and the early printing of classical texts.